WILD ESSENCE

*Return to the Peace & Freedom
of Your Inner Wilderness*

JODI SKY ROGERS

BALBOA.
PRESS

A DIVISION OF HAY HOUSE

Balboa Press books may be ordered through booksellers or by contacting:

Balboa Press
A Division of Hay House
1663 Liberty Drive
Bloomington, IN 47403
www.balboapress.com
1 (877) 407-4847

Because of the dynamic nature of the Internet, any web addresses or
links contained in this book may have changed since publication and
may no longer be valid. The views expressed in this work are solely those
of the author and do not necessarily reflect the views of the publisher,
and the publisher hereby disclaims any responsibility for them.

The author of this book does not dispense medical advice or prescribe the use
of any technique as a form of treatment for physical, emotional, or medical
problems without the advice of a physician, either directly or indirectly. The
intent of the author is only to offer information of a general nature to help
you in your quest for emotional and spiritual well-being. In the event you use
any of the information in this book for yourself, which is your constitutional
right, the author and the publisher assume no responsibility for your actions.

Any people depicted in stock imagery provided by Thinkstock are
models, and such images are being used for illustrative purposes only.
Certain stock imagery © Thinkstock.

Printed in the United States of America.

ISBN: 978-1-4525-9857-4 (sc)
ISBN: 978-1-4525-9858-1 (e)

Balboa Press rev. date: 11/21/2014

DEDICATION

To all the Wild Women in my life
To the late Stephanie Rae Gerke, a beautiful
wild soul who is forever in my heart

Contents

PREFACE

This book is about coming home to your Self and connecting with the creative and divine essence within. It explores how you can loosen the grips of the barriers that diminish you and keep you trapped, barriers that disconnect you from your inner essence. So many women, myself included, struggle with both the external and internal shackles that set out to tame and cage their inner essence. Drawing from my own experiences, I've recognized the need to remind the women of the world whose souls have been broken in to submission, that they are essentially wild creatures of profound beauty who are meant to *be* and express all of who they are, not lurk in the shadows. You have incredible gifts to share that are of great value to all of us. Self-expression and self-realization are your birthright.

The seed for the Wild Essence book germinated when I asked myself two questions, 'What makes me feel free and uninhibited?' and 'What stands in the way of me being who I am fully?' When I examined what stands in my way, it was very clear that my barriers stem from the stories and beliefs created by my negative experiences that I still project onto myself internally. On the subject of what makes me feel free, along with noticing that I am most at peace in moments of stillness, when I live from my heart space or when I focus on the things or experiences that inspire me, I also recognized that I feel most alive when I'm immersed in the beauty of the wild Earth. I find so much inspiration and healing from Mother Earth. Through my connection with Nature my soul is nurtured. I've become acquainted with the idea of the Divine Feminine and discovered the love of the Goddess in the wilderness. It occurred to me that perhaps the wilderness makes me feel so alive and attuned to Spirit because it is an outward projection of the inner essence alive within the center of my being – my wild essence. The wild Earth is a reflection of the abundance, vibrancy and untamed nature of our unlimited inner spirit. For that reason, wilderness became my metaphor for spiritual peace and freedom. This book therefore also includes intricately woven threads of wild whispers, insights and analogies from Nature.

Wild Essence puts forward that walking a spiritual path and reconnecting with the inner wilderness is like an un-taming of a domesticated heart and restoring one's soul to its freest and most natural form. I share some of the experiences, lessons and helpful approaches that have brought me to a place of healing, peace and freedom on my journey with the intention to assist you on your own journey as you reclaim a deeper connection with your inner wilds.

How to use the Mantras and Meditations

The end of each chapter includes a list of mantras and a written guided meditation. They're meant to help you integrate new uplifting beliefs that nurture your connection with your wild essence. Mantras are simple one line positive affirmations that can be used daily in a manner that best suites you. They help you to shift from negative thought patterns to positive ones. You can recite them in the mornings and evenings, or throughout the day. You can write them down on small pieces of cardboard or paper. Then pin these on your vision board, use them as a journal bookmark, stick them on your mirror, or place them wherever you will see them often, stop and read them. The mantras can also be shared as quotes on Twitter, Facebook or Instagram.

The written guided meditations are longer than the mantras and are designed for peaceful self-reflection. I'd recommend reading through them one or two times to get acquainted with it before doing the meditation. You can start or end your day with a meditation. Find a quiet place where you will have some personal space and can get comfortable when you meditate. If possible, ensure that you will not be disturbed. Feel free to light some candles or play some soothing music to create a relaxing environment. It may be helpful to keep a process journal with you where you can write down any insights that surface when you work with the meditations and mantras. Try to do each meditation at the end of the relevant chapter at least once before moving on to the next.

May this book bring you peace, freedom and the magic of your wild inner treasures!

1

WILD ESSENCE

'We are born of sky, stars, and spirit, yet when we meld into physical form, we forget the far-reaching mystery that dwells in our depths.'
~ **Denise Linn**

I look up at the star studded sky over the African bushveld as diamonds twinkle against the black blanket of night. There is no moon tonight, only the primal call of lions and jackal that echoes from unseen places in the dark. The palpable sense of mystery suspended in the warm evening air leaves me with the impression that this is the land that Spirit made at the beginning of time. Some pieces of wild Earth feel as timeless as our souls when they are unaltered by the hand of man. In my mind's eye, I conjure up images of the ancients roaming these grassy plains in a period long past and forgotten. I see their phantom silhouettes sitting and dancing around the crackling fire, telling the stories that time has passed down through their bloodlines. Perhaps thousands of years ago they stood looking up at the same sky on a moonless night, writing the stories of the land in the stars – Orion's Belt cast in the role of three zebras and Pleiades playing the daughters of the sky gods - as Bushmen mythology tells.

"There is nothing more beautiful than this," my thoughts whisper as I listen to the sound of noctivagant creatures.

It's been a wonderful evening. Just hours ago I watched the last sunset of the year melt across the tranquil grasslands and the sun dissolve into its slumber before we headed down to the communal boma of the game lodge for an intimate gathering to honor the festivities of the occasion. For a couple years now, I've had the privilege of seeing in the New Year with my husband and a close circle of cherished friends in the 'cathedral of the wild' as conservationist Boyd Varty calls it. The ambience is so relaxed and we've enjoyed great food, conversations and lots of full bellied laughs. Since we've been coming here, I can't imagine being anywhere else. Usually I am so focused on ushering in another year and wondering what it will bring my way. This time, as the sun set on 2013, I took a moment of solitude to honor what has been, both the blessings for which I am grateful and the struggles that I've failed to accept. I exhaled and released it all. What has been has been. *"May what is lost be forgotten or returned to me in a new form if it is meant to,"* I said quietly in my heart. I felt a sense of relief as I did.

Tomorrow is a fresh day and life begins anew. Tomorrow I will set new intentions for what I want in my life. The first day of the year falls on the New Moon, which according to Celtic mystic traditions is the perfect time to plant new seeds and wishes for future manifestation. For now, I let it all go, surrendering the way a leaf does when it falls from a tree in the Fall or Autumn as we call it here in South Africa. For now, I listen to the breath of the bush as it breathes to the rhythm of the stars. Away from the city lights, glitzy outfits, smoky nightclubs and futile attempts at searching for the perfect New Year's party, the magic of the bush makes me feel so connected to Spirit and attuned to the flow of the Universe. Here, meditation and moments of profound insight come easier. I feel more able to release restrictions and flow at a different pace of life, a pace that feels more natural and easy. I figure it has something to do with how the wilderness mirrors my own wild nature. It allows me to connect with my inner wilderness – the untamed essence of my Spirit.

The mystery of the wild reaches deep within to touch uncharted scapes inside of me. Nature has a hard exterior that can make one perceive it as harsh, destructive or violent. But when you delve below the surface, you find its softness – a delicate interior that emanates a hush of beauty, stillness and sacred wisdom. Its softness wants to hold us in warm embraces of wild comfort, and to teach us its divine ways of being, the way of the heart. I find threads of this holy beauty in the wild whispers echoed by the wind as falcons, buzzards, pin-tailed whydahs and shrikes take flight against the azure summer sky. There is a beautiful chaos in how the guinea fowls and wild hare dart through the dry grasses. The same beauty is found in the sound of springbuck, zebra and wildebeest herds galloping across the grasslands. Watching these animals roaming freely in their natural habitat is such a gift. There is something so magical about the way the afternoon sun trickles through the leaves of the thorny acacia trees and the feel of a butterfly wing gently brushing against my cheek as it flutters past me in search of blossoms and nectar.

Precious moments of stillness in places like this open me up. They make me see clearly that like the wilderness around me, there is a beautiful place inside of me that is wild. The wild essence that I see when I peer into the ocean of unhindered peace resting in the eyes of eland also rests at my center. That place exists in you too. It is in the midst of your wild essence that the fires of desire burn brightly and unapologetically if given the chance. This is where the dreamer in you dwells, hungry for the adventure of living life fully and thirstily drinking sweet nectar from your serene center. It is home to the mender who helps your jaded soul find peace and restoration in times of need. It is home to the wise sage, the mighty priestess and the succulent wild woman – all aspects of the psyche that are alive in you.

The untamed beauty that you see around you in Nature is a mirror of who you really are. Spiritual teachers such as Dr. Wayne Dyer, Doreen Virtue and Sonia Choquette will remind you that you were born a perfect and beautiful child of the Universe and that you are an incredible embodiment of Divine love and light. This is what we all are. As a unique and creative soul, you are equipped with all that you need to sparkle and create amazing things in your life. When you own your wild essence and show up for life, then major shifts occur in your experience and magic happens. It's funny how easily we forget this. We forget who we are. We forget that, as philosopher Pierre Teilhard de Chardin so aptly put it, *'We are spiritual beings having a physical experience.'*

The Universe always wants you to remember. In the eloquent words of self-starter Danielle LaPorte, the Universe keeps asking you, *'Can you remember who you were before the world told you who you should be?'* So it sends you reminders, clues and sacred messages to decode. In instances of stillness when you stop searching and allow yourself to be, these sacred messages and reminders permeate your consciousness. They unveil themselves in your life in various ways – through people, in places that you explore and experiences that unfold around you. They find you as signs, synchronicities and miracles which remind you that a greater power is at play. In my world, more often than not I've found them in Mother Nature. The wild Earth writes love letters on the fine threads of each feather that drifts gracefully to the Earth. I find maps to my inner treasures encoded in the veins of each leaf. Each message leaves me wondering, *'How much more amazing would the world be if I gave myself permission to let my wild essence shine?'* Can you imagine the impact that allowing yourself to be who you are fully would have on your life and the world? The answer is so obvious it may even come across as cliché because the likelihood is that you would have heard it several times before, yet I feel compelled to reinforce this beautiful message – Liberating your wild essence would have a profound impact on your life and the world, because something of such tremendous value would be returned to its rightful place in the greater scheme of things.

So why then do we often struggle to retain such an important understanding and keep it at the forefront of our minds? Years of self-examination, as well as delving into various spiritual and metaphysical philosophies have led me to believe that this can be attributed to the way in which we are socialized and how we learn to think about ourselves. When babies are born, we are in awe of their magnificent beauty and vulnerability. Yet, as they grow, they learn to feel less and less perfect because of the self-limiting beliefs projected onto them by the people who influence their perceptions of themselves and society as a whole.

I remember a time in my childhood that was blissful. I spent my days running wild, playing in the garden, climbing trees and collecting tadpoles down by the river. It felt as though I had a lifetime of adventures exploring the hills and valleys, collecting wild flowers and digging for quartz crystals. In those times, my wild essence was free and my sense of wonder navigated me through my days. The world was full of possibilities, my dreams were big and I believed in my potential to do anything. Unfortunately, the older I got, the more things began to change. New rules and codes of conduct were set in place in my home and in my life. I was introduced to new limits that told me there was no place for my dreams. As I discovered, growing up meant denying my inner essence and behaving in 'acceptable' ways. Suddenly there was a new memo as to what I could and couldn't do. Often it felt as though any bit of personal freedom that my wild essence desired was being taken away. I was no longer able to go adventuring in the natural outdoor world as much as I used to. Wasn't it a common perception that good girls stayed home, did their homework, behaved like ladies and helped their mothers with chores around the house after all?

Around about that time, the dynamics of my life shifted drastically. The world became a restrictive and toxic place where I was frequently subjected to emotional, mental and sometimes physical abuse. In the beginning the rebel in me resisted as much and as often as possible. But at each attempt, it felt as though the abusers and bullies who entered my environment made a point of reining me in and attempted to break my spirit. I was constantly harassed, berated, belittled and threatened. Few days went by without me being reminded of how inadequate I was. I grew up hearing things like 'You are useless.' 'You're so ugly and stupid.' and 'You will never amount to anything in life.' One of the most common mantras directed at me over and over again was, 'Today, I'm going to make your life hell. I'm going to make you wish that you were dead.' As a consequence, I felt trapped. I never felt safe or free to be myself. I was unable to express my thoughts or feelings. Gradually, I went from being a bubbly wild child to being quiet, scared, withdrawn and depressed. Eventually I felt that those suppressive and abusive personalities had won the battle because I did live in some kind of hell and I did wish that I was dead too.

Nature was my escape and safe haven when dealing with the unpredictability and conflict in my life at a young age. Yet, as if symbolically mirroring the internal process that was coming into play, as I entered a life stage where my wild spirit was being tamed, domesticated and broken down, externally I was largely cut off from a wild world of Nature that I loved so much too. For the most part, I was limited to the confines of the walls of our home. Something about the exprerience makes me think of an excerpt from the Diary of Anais Nin where she describes her arrival in New York. Anais wrote: *"…the ship began to move again, slowly, as though she approached the great city with fear. Now, leaning on the railing, I couldn't hear anything…Huge buildings went by in front of me. I hated those buildings in advance because they hid what I love most--flowers, birds, fields, liberty."*

A part of my thinks that like many young souls, her repulsion at those buildings was just as much about the death of her innocence and inner wilds as it was about her love for the wild things of the Earth.

If dealing with the difficult dynamics of my changing life was not enough, another layer of manacles were added to the mix. That was being born into the oppressive era of apartheid. This meant being denied opportunities, confined to particular areas and denied access to facilities, beaches, shops, restaurants, etc., on the basis of our skin color. I was a little more fortunate to grow up in a time when things were changing, so I did not experience being racially abused, reduced, dehumanized and fed lies about inferiority as severely as my parents, grandparents and older generations did. However, the residue was still enough to leave a negative impact on my perception of myself and my abilities.

These are the kinds of experiences that my wild essence has survived on my journey. Each of our lives is different, with some of us facing more harsh circumstances than others. Regardless of the details of your experiences, we can all identify with the process of disconnecting from our inner wilderness due to the restrictive limitations of parenting, relationships, religious communities, political influences or society in general being projected onto us on some level. It is a Universal story. Humanity has created an ego-centric world where the magnificence of your wild essence is suppressed. Your inner wilderness thus becomes domesticated by the conditioning of your upbringing and society. Instead of being who you are completely, you have to constantly battle to just be yourself without being judged or rejected. Consequently, you lose touch with your true self and often internalize the critical voices and beliefs that others project onto you. You learn to project them onto yourself and the people in your life too. In the end, you only embody a fraction of your incredible wild essence and you are left feeling disconnected from your soul, living an inauthentic life in a dispirited world. As women, we often feel the brunt of this domestication process more acutely, especially when you are exposed to patriarchal or chauvinistic belief systems.

Fortunately outdated paradigms that people around the world have adhered to for so long are shifting. Outmoded thought systems are collapsing and a wave of transformation that was catalyzed by courageous souls, dreamers, change makers and trail blazers has carried us into a time of conscious evolution. We have entered into the era of living authentic lives rooted in our wild essences. As a result, a mass spirit wilding is taking place, one where you and so many of the people around you are reconnecting to their heart space and returning to the peace and freedom of their inner wilderness. When you look closely, you will see the evidence of this transformation taking place in yourself and in others around you too. By living from this wild and heart-centered space, you are able see the importance of releasing the barriers that have kept you from being who you truly are. Your transformations may be big and bold or small quiet ones. Perhaps the wild whispers of your heart are calling you to honor yourself by releasing a job that you hate or to walk away from an abusive relationship and to reinvent your life completely. Perhaps these whispers surface as the urge to take the island holiday that you've always dreamed of, or to go on that yoga retreat in Bali. Or they could be subtle things like giving yourself space to breathe, space for a quiet moment to watch the sunrise, space to listen to the sound of the waves, alone time to draw a hot bubble bath or permission to love and accept yourself as you are. Regardless of how these whispers manifest in your life, you are learning to make different choices – ones that allow you to turn away from a fear-based consciousness and to place your faith and energy in the light of love instead. People all around you, including you, feel called to carve out a life that resonates with their soul. You recognize that the wisdom of your wild essence has the power to inform your life choices and guide you to your highest good. As this new world starts taking form, you are no longer able to ignore your heart's wild whispers. You are no longer able to ignore your dreams and deep soul desires. Living an authentic life aligned to your soul's truth and pursuing your life purpose is more important now than ever before. Your wild essence asks you to see the sacred beauty of Spirit that is alive in you and in all life. It compels you to love yourself enough to make decisions that serve your highest good, as well as the highest good of all. It gives you the vision to recognize that by setting your wild spirit free and making new choices not only do you change your life but you also contribute to changing the world for the better. How awesome is that!

Allowing your wild essence the space to be is an important part of heart-centered living that leads to beautiful periods of unfolding. However, the experiences I've had on my spiritual journey have shown me that the process of unshackling and releasing the things and beliefs that restrict you is also a significant part of the process. In fact, it is integral in returning to the peace and freedom of your wild essence. I've therefore come to see walking my spiritual path as a form of re-wilding. To re-wild means to return something to its natural state of wilderness, to bring back missing pieces that once occurred naturally in a space that has been altered. I think that this is exactly what you do when you break down negative internal barriers to bring your wild essence to the fore. Removing the things that diminish your personal power can be a grueling process. In fact, it's been the most challenging part of my journey thus far. But each step I've taken has brought me one step closer to my essence. As I continue to explore the expanses of my inner wilderness, I find new shackles to shed. I see my wild essence un-cage more and more when I trade negative thought patterns in for new beliefs, situations and experiences that set my heart alight with love and inspiration. My hope is that the experiences and insights that I share in this book will shed light on your experiences in some way, regardless of where you are in your personal journey.

♥

~ Mantra Moment ~

(Tweet, Instagram, Share on Facebook
#wildessence #jodiskyrogers)

♥

"There is a beautiful place inside of me that is Wild."

♥

"My wild essence embodies Divine love and light."

♥

**"When you own your wild essence and
show up for life, then major shifts occur in
your experience and magic happens."**

♥

"I give myself permission to let my wild essence shine."

♥

Meditation: Meet Your Wild Essence

Close your eyes. Take a few deep breaths, in and out.

Feel yourself relaxing as you do. Let go of any thoughts or worries. Allow yourself to be present in the moment as you continue to breathe deeply for a few more moments.

Now focus your attention on your center and the space around your solar plexus. Feel into this place intuitively. Notice a sphere of white light radiating from your center. As you focus on the sphere of light within you, you feel a deep sense of love and calm envelope you.

See the sphere of light expanding, growing bigger and bigger as it spreads throughout your body. The peace and love grow in you as the light expands.

This light is the essence of who you truly are – an embodiment of the Divine. Be present with your true essence and notice how free and liberating it feels.

Notice the serene sense of calm that your natural essence emanates.

Notice its wildness and how freely the energy flows when you allow your wild essence to open up and expand. Bask in this feeling for as long as you need to.

When you are ready, return your focus to your breathing, taking a deep breath in and out.

Be present in your body, feel your hands and your feet. Then open your eyes.

♥

2

Your Unknown Wilds

"The fear of an unknown never resolves, because the
unknown expands infinitely outward, leaving you to
cling pitifully to any small shelter of the known..."
~ Caroline Kettlewell

For so long I'd dreamt of having this freedom. The freedom
to wake up in a life molded to the vision of my dreams. I
yearned to start my days in sacred communion with the
Earth, meditating on mystery and feeling the tender caress
of Spirit in the early morning breeze. I'd longed for days
filled with doing meaningful work aligned to my spiritual
path and life purpose. Yet here I am, with the freedom to
do, to live and to be in a way that resonates so strongly with
my wild essence and still for reasons that I can't understand
I am keeping myself confined by the walls of domestication.

While I have the freedom to roam the city, explore its wild
spaces and have new experiences, I keep myself trapped
in my home, believing that I need to work first, build an
empire perhaps before I am afforded the luxury of a freer

life. While I have the freedom to structure my day in a way that nurtures my soul and stokes the fires of my creativity, I impose rigid work hours and rules pretty much the same as in any formal workplace. I find my days occupied with 'busy' work, yet I'm not really being productive. At the end of the day, I am exhausted and start freaking out about not doing enough, not being enough and not getting my new healing business off the ground fast enough. And then when I reach breaking point, I feel as though I am on the cusp of something, standing at the garden gate looking down the path that leads to the wilderness of my soul. Somehow it makes me think of the opening lines of Bod Dylan's song, 'Isis', where he sings about riding into *"the wild unknown country"*. Yet, although I've craved a life centered in the lush wild essence for so long, now that I am standing in front of it, I don't have the courage to venture out of the familiar confines of domestication and into my wild unknown territory. A strange sense of déjà vu lingers as I come to this realization. Then I remember that I have been here before. I am taken back to a period in my life several years prior when I was doing a walking meditation on the beach. I recall the experience so vividly:

The cool ocean breeze caressed my skin. It was an instant relief to the summer heat. Centered in a walking meditation, I closed my eyes and let my spirit guide me. I felt the sand give way under the weight of my feet, molding the memory of my presence in it as I slowly took one step after the next. Each time I heard the waves wash in, fear stirred in the darkness behind my shut eyelids. Each time the cool sea water washed over my feet, I was taken by surprise. I challenged myself not to open my eyes.

"Trust," I said. "Let your Spirit guide each step."

Occasionally, I gave in and opened my eyes to ensure that the path before me was clear and safe. When I reached a rock in my path, I decided to sit down next to it. Facing the ocean, I closed my eyes once more and continued the sensory meditation. I listened to the sound of the ocean and felt the salt spray on my skin. My soul danced to the rhythm of the waves as the wind whispered sweet stories of mermaids, sailors and forgotten sorrows.

I felt so peaceful. Yet still, each time I heard the waves coming in, fear rose in me even though I knew that by the time the water reached me it would barely tickle my toes. I turned my attention to this fear and the wise inner spark in me began to see that it was the all-too-familiar fear of the unknown. The Unknown, that which either cannot be seen, touched or fully understood. That which must always be treated with mistrust, or so we are taught. Behind closed eyes, the ocean was a big, unpredictable and somewhat scary creature. Unwilling to trust, my ego dreamt up all kinds of possible threats to my safety. And then it hit me...my ego-based mind perceived my spiritual essence in pretty much the same way that it saw the ocean in that moment. It viewed my Spirit as something wild, unpredictable and unknown. Because of this, a part of me was not ready to trust my Spirit to steer my path...

"I need the sea because it teaches me" ~ Pablo Neruda

Dreams are windows into the state our souls. Sometimes our consciousness sorts through the mundane occurrences of daily life in the dream plain. Other times, they bring symbolic messages that the subconscious needs our awareness to comprehend. The experience that I had on the beach was followed by a series of dreams which brought me face to face with my resistance to my own wild essence. First, I dreamt that I was visiting a beautiful day spa. The spa had stunning gardens, swimming pools, statues of spiritual deities and koi ponds. The garden was vibrant and full of color. Birdsong sounded in the air. While waiting for my massage, I decided to explore the gardens. Walking around, I reached the edge of the property where I found a narrow doorway. I walked through it and on the other side I discovered vast expanses of rock and dense forest. Intrigued, I so wanted to explore the wilderness before me, but something in me was afraid. I took a few steps forward. A thrill of excitement washed over me, but still fear held me back. So I stopped. I heard a voice calling me to come deeper into the wilderness to explore. I thought about it for a moment, eager, yet hesitant at the same time. In the end, my fear of the unknown got the better of me. I went back to the confines of the garden and I felt disappointed in myself for not mustering the courage to explore. Upon waking, I realized that the dream was calling me to reconnoiter the spiritual wilderness within – my deeper consciousness and essential self. The idea of it clearly terrified my ego-based self. As if to make sure that I got it, I was sent yet another dream to reinforce the same message a few nights later. This time, I dreamt that I was in a glass house boat drifting over the ocean. I looked down at the glass floor and what I saw was incredible. Whales, dolphins and colorful tropical fish were swimming in the sparkling turquoise water below. It was the most breath-taking thing to watch and I spent a few long moments marveling at the sight of it all. I wanted to jump into the ocean and swim freely with the amazing aquatic life. I went out onto the deck, intending to dive in, but stopped myself. That fearful little egoic voice in my head said *"No, it's safer to stay in the confines of the glass boat. You can't trust the wild unpredictable ocean."* Yet again, I gave in to fear and awoke feeling disappointed.

When you've become acquainted with the beauty of your wild essence, fearing it seems like an illogical thing to do. Yet, as I found during the beach meditation and the period that followed, I feared venturing into my inner wilderness. That was the first time I caught a glimpse of the idea of the unfamiliarity of my own wild essence. It brought home an important understanding, one that set in motion a new phase in my spiritual unfolding. Through my quest to understand why I was afraid to surrender into the loving embrace of the Divine and my own essence, I began to recognize just how the confines of domestication along with the effects of conditioning and the resultant self-defeating behavior had influenced my experiences. I'd read about social conditioning and self-defeating behavior in various psychology and self-help books. But it wasn't until I became acquainted with these concepts on a deeply personal level that I saw how it was keeping my wild essence tamed.

I now saw firsthand how from our earliest days we are channeled in the direction of social conformity through conditioning or indoctrination in one form or another. The experiences and the influences in our formative years create an identity, patterns and beliefs that inform how we live in the world. Not all conditioning is bad. As human beings we develop by means of learnt behavior. Our parents and community raise us by transferring education and behavioral patterns. So some form of conditioning, to enforce an understanding of how to survive and interact with the rest of society in healthy ways, is necessary. However, one of the things that I learnt when I trained as a Life Coach is that the negative form of conditioning appears when self-limiting and often irrational belief systems are transferred consciously or subconsciously. Authors and Coaches such as Louise Hay, Cheryl Richardson and Martha Beck often explain that these kinds of limiting beliefs bring about restrictive situations that stifle your personal growth and ability to live your life in a way that supports and nurtures your wild essence. They shape how you manifest your reality. For the most part of our lives, we are encouraged to play it safe, to toe the line and to color within the borders of what is deemed socially acceptable. Your wild essence is bent and beaten into shape, groomed to play a role that your family, your community and society see fit for you. You learn to censor yourself and put your true desires aside to please others instead. In many cases we are taught to ignore our own needs. Across the ages man has had an obsession with taming Nature. To my mind, the conditioning that we experience through the way that we are socialized is no different to the way that Nature is tamed, dominated and domesticated.

"In a world that generally regards refinement and domestication of everything from sugar to human instincts to be the hallmark of civilization and progress, we need to be mindful that invariably something has been lost in the process." ~ Ian McCallum

Author, Ian McCallum, highlights in his book, 'Ecological Intelligence', that something precious is lost when the wild essence of your being is shackled. The authentic nature of one's Spirit is extinguished. Your creative spirit is subdued and you become stuck in uninspiring routines doing the same thing in the same way over and over again. Captivity kills the Spirit and alters the true nature of any being. It's little wonder that fireflies don't survive long in captivity. They may be okay and light up in your jar for a day or two, but longer than that they don't stand a chance. Your dreams don't survive long in a captive heart either. They were not meant to exist that way. When stuffed away for too long, they die, locking us into a lifetime of grief as we mourn the things that could have been. This is the root of melancholic conditions such as depression for many people. People and dreams thrive in their natural habitat out in the world. This is the best place to admire their warm glow from. When wild creatures, both animal and human, are captured and caged, they lose touch with their natural instincts. Unable to express their authentic wild spirit, they inhabit a limited existence. They express only a minute fragment of their full capacity or creative essence.

Because of this domestication, your magnificent Spirit is often shut away in a dark cave within. The burning fires of desire are starved for air. Your truths silenced. You learn to believe that the essential self – the willful, intuitive, imaginative and powerful inner Spirit – is something to be suppressed and shunned. Resting in the darkness, that inner wilderness transforms into a *wild unknown* territory or unknown wilderness of sorts. Just like the ocean in my walking meditation, your truest and most natural self becomes unfamiliar and in turn, something to be feared.

After the epiphany that the beach meditation led me to, I was painfully aware of the restrictive existence that I'd etched out for myself. During that period of my life, I was deepening my spirituality and I'd begun working with crystals, energy healing and angel therapy. It was a beautiful and exciting time and my spirit was blooming. I was beginning to have profound spiritual experiences, synchronicities showed up everywhere and things that didn't resonate with me where falling away. At the same time, I was experiencing some intense resistance. Although I wasn't always fully cognizant of it, a big part of me was holding back. Examining the underbelly of the resistance to my wild essence revealed various layers to my own story. Even though I was expanding my awareness, growing spiritually and on a beautiful journey of self-discovery, I still clung to old barriers and the self-limiting beliefs. I carried so much fear. I also carried all of the voices who told me that I was worthless and would never do anything of value with my life. I held on to so much past pain. The scars that past abuse, hurt and rejection left on my psyche still needed healing. Connecting to my inner self often startled me, because I believed that I had no right to express my authentic spirit.

After all, who was I to be bigger than life had permitted me to be? That very question is a prime example of the types of limiting beliefs that we absorb, internalize and use to keep the inner self small. Slowly, I began to find the resources and healing support that I needed to peel away those restrictive internal barriers layer by layer. I went for healing sessions, counseling, life-coaching and attended spiritual retreats. I read self-help and spiritual books. I trained in various metaphysical modalities and worked hard to find peace by creating a self-nurturing daily spiritual practice. As usual, a great deal of my healing and spiritual insights came from spending time in Nature. And I lived happily ever after... Or so I thought.

Here I am in pretty much the same space – full of fear of the unknown and feeling caged by restrictive patterns that I keep reinforcing. It is not my job or anyone else who is keeping me captive. I am doing it to myself.

"Why am I doing this?" I wonder.

"Sometimes something needs to crack before something new is born." ~ Jane Lee Logan

I remind myself that I've begun one of the most exciting adventures in my life. It's a very liberating step to finally gather the courage to release the shackles of an unfulfilling job and toxic working environment. I am putting the needs of my wild essence first and following my soul's guidance to pursue a path more meaningful to me. For a long time, I'd been planning and taking steps to plunge into the life that I'd dreamed of – working as a spiritual healer, coach and writer. Now, here I am embarking on this new journey, heeding to that inner call to walk this spiritual path and responding to what my soul is aching for, but still I am unhappy. Still I feel stuck. Still I do not know how to be free and at peace. In a moment of self-reflection, I am able to see why I've landed myself in this rut. Thinking back to when my big life change kicked off, I recall how that period was filled with wonderful days where everything flowed. I woke up excited. I was full of energy and grateful for the opportunity to work at building my dream. Of course, there were also times when nothing seemed to go right. Those moments were not so easy, but they allowed me to try different things, to expand my horizons and to learn about what worked for me, as well as what worked for my clients when it came to my business. But at some point, something else came into play. For one thing, I realize that I am maintaining my 9-5 desk job mindset, trying to sit at a desk for 12 to 14 hours, designing services, marketing, advertising, writing and networking online. I realize that I am being too rigid by trying to apply tried and trusted work methods that don't apply to my new career path. Structure has its place, but it seems to be stifling my creativity in this instance. I need the freedom to try different things and learn to think of my work differently as well.

My spirit has been guiding me on what steps to take, but I also now see how I was afraid to hand control over to my wild essence, because I was unsure of where it was taking me. I recognize that I was struggling to trust and flow in the direction that guidance was steering me towards because the uncertainly of it all scared me. Although I am no longer a victim of past experiences or feeling stuck in an unhappy job, the residue of domestication is still very much alive in my unconscious mind in the form of self-defeating patterns at this point. It seems that the more space I've been giving my essence in my life, the more internal resistance I experience. In hindsight I recognize that it wasn't sudden. The sneaky little mud monsters of self-doubt, self-criticism and fear lurked in the shadows, slowly grabbing at me here and there. What started as occasional little voices that said "This will never work", "You're not good enough", "You're useless", "You've made a big mistake", "Your stupid dream has no place in the real world", gradually became louder and more frequent over time, until eventually I found myself completely pulled into a swamp of shadows and disconnected from my wild essence. The more I ponder my predicament, the more the wisdom of my essence shows me how giving into fear has allowed me to cling to the familiar chains of internal confinement and to uphold the restrictive barriers of domestication that I was used to.

I am somewhat taken by surprise with what I discover in my reflection, because I self-righteously believed that after spending a number of years connecting with my inner world, healing, doing release work and rebuilding my sense of self, I was at the point of my life where I'd worked through most of my internal stumbling blocks. I wasn't expecting to encounter parts of myself that I thought were long healed, only to find that there were more layers of negative conditioning to shed. I guess that is the beauty of the journey. As Louise Hay so aptly put it, 'there are always new layers to peel away'.

While sorting things out in my head and trying to figure out a way forward, I spend an afternoon reading poetry and inspiring texts to uplift my spirit when I come across Mary Oliver's poem Wild Geese. In the first few lines of the beautiful piece this incredible poet speaks of not having to struggle or suffer, but instead just to allow oneself to align with what your wild essence loves and requires to simply *be*. Perhaps it's because it had been such a long time since I'd read these words, but suddenly I am moved to a moment of clarity. Aside from the fear of my inner self, I'm caught up in a struggle, because that is all I know. Part of me believes that I have to struggle to justify my right to be or live my best life. I am struggling against the natural flow of things, trying hard to be a certain idea of who I'm supposed to be. It's almost as if I am punishing myself for heeding my calling and waiting for someone out there to give me permission to ease up on myself. Yet, what I really need to do is allow myself to be who I am. I need to give myself permission to be me. That permission doesn't come from anyone else. I need to give myself permission to *'let the soft animal of my body'* or my wild essence *'love what it loves'*, as Mary Oliver puts it in the poem. How often do we spend time waiting for someone else to give us the permission to be our authentic selves? Why do we feel that our lives, or our needs and dreams are only justified if some unknown outer source says that they are? The truth is that these things are your birthright. The only permission you need is your own.

So I set the intention to give myself that permission, deciding that from this point forward I will allow and flow, not resist, fear and struggle. I tell myself to take a positive outlook on this and to see it as an opportunity to dive deeper inward, rather than a setback. I set the intention to use this as an opportunity to take some time out for healing and to release my barriers. I commit to finding ways to love, accept myself fully and to step into a centered place that holds a higher vibration. Just as I come to this decision, my husband and I receive news from our landlady that she is planning to sell the apartment that we have been renting for the past 6 years. We will need to move out in three months. The timing is perfect. We have already started looking for a new place because we wanted more space, a therapy room for my clients and a garden. I feel as though this timely news is a push in the right direction that gives me permission to put my healing business on hold until we are settled in a new place. For three months, as I pack up my life and my home, I also purge the past and release my limitations. It is an emotional and sometimes difficult process, but when I remind myself that these barriers are all illusions, they become easier to shed.

Mystic poet Rumi once wrote that, *'Your task is not to seek for love, but merely to seek and find all the barriers within yourself that you have built against it.'*

I now understand what he meant. The walls of domestication, the conditioning and those self-defeating patterns only cage your creative essence. It snuffs out your incredible wild soul and cuts you off from the infinite well of love and light within. But when you step into your personal power and begin to peel away these blocks and layers, you become present with the heart-centered love of your wild essence.

In the midst of the chaotic changes and internal work, I find gentle ways to be more present. I meditate more, journal and go for energy healing sessions. I take relaxing baths and lie in the tub with a good book at midday after a long morning of packing and sorting things. I take leisurely strolls around the neighborhood that I am leaving. I spend more time enjoying the Spring-time outdoors going on hikes. As I do, I feel the peace of my wild essence returning to the center of my life to navigate my path.

♥

~ Mantra Moment ~

(Tweet, Instagram, Share on Facebook
#wildessence #jodiskyrogers)

♥

"I am not my past. I choose to release the barriers and beliefs that limit me."

♥

"My wild essence is a source of Divine guidance and wisdom."

♥

"It is safe for me to trust the guidance of my spiritual essence."

♥

Meditation: Uncover the Resistance to Your Wild Essence

Find a quiet place where you can get comfortable and will not be disturbed. Take a few deep breaths, close your eyes and center yourself.

When you are present in a peaceful state, then connect with your Wild Essence the same way that you did in the previous meditation. Spend a few moments resting in the loving light of your wild essence.

Notice if any feelings of fear around your wild essence arise. Are you resisting your inner wilderness in any way? Pay attention to what comes up.

Where in your body do you feel this resistance or fear? If it had a physical form, what shape would it be? What color would it be?

Ask the resistance where it stems from. What triggers it? Listen to any thoughts or answers that surface when you do.

Now take a moment to breathe through the resistance or fear as you say: "I release my fear. I release the pattern in me that is creating this resistance."

Breathe in and then let it all go as you exhale. As you do, feel your wild essence expand.

When you are ready to conclude the meditation, bring your attention back to your body. Feel your fingers and your toes. Open your eyes.

3

Demystifying the Unknown Wilderness

"...there's a silent voice in the wilderness that we hear only when no one else is around. When you go far, far beyond, out across the netherlands of the Known, the din of human static slowly fades away..."
~ Rob Schultheis

The summer rain falls gently and splashes against the ground like delicate hooves of unseen deer whose ghosts are dancing beneath the trees. It smells like my childhood. The sounds of Nature rest gently in my ears, like soothing lullabies sung softly to me by the Great Mother. In the distance I hear the quiet rumble of thunder. The taste of fresh mystery hangs in the air like a thick layer of honey ready to be licked up by willing souls who go out into the rain in search of something sacred. I sit on the grass to meditate. I feel the nurturing support of the Earth below me – solid, firm, yet comfortable. Beside me, the tall wise Eucalyptus and Blue Gum trees stand in silence. Being in their presence is so calming. They emanate the deep contentment of peace and I can't help but drop into the stillness of my own center, inevitably mirroring that peace back to them. A family of mischievous Vervet monkeys pounce from branch to branch, curiously watching me perch in lotus position. The fine raindrops that have been moistening my skin slowly dissipate as the flocculent clouds overhead begin to open up, revealing a touch of pale blue sky. The mist in the valley around the cabin is lifting too. I am grateful because this brief summer drizzle means cool and easy weather for the morning hike up to the ruins.

The ancient stone ruins in the South African Highlands of Mpumalanga are the subject of much speculation. From an aerial view of the area one would see hundreds of these primitive stone wall circles scattered across the landscape. Archaeologists don't seem to have come to a precise consensus about their origins and who is responsible for creating them. Some attribute the existence of their complex settlements to the early baKoni people, an Nguni tribe who settled in the area around the early 18th century. Others say that like the Great Zimbabwean ruins, these ruins are remnants of ancient mines connected to a primeval civilization. I've heard stories that this proposed civilization had links with ancient Sumerian, Yemen, Egyptian and Chinese cultures who were rumored to have come South to mine gold. According to scientist and author Michael Tellinger, some of the monoliths nearby which are aligned on the same longitudinal line as Great Zimbabwe and the Great Pyramids are 75,000 years old, which he says sets their origins in a period consistent with the rise of Orion's belt.

The shroud of mystery surrounding the ruins is fascinating, so I am pretty excited to be exploring them myself. Silent observers and relics of abandoned worlds unknown to us, the timeless lichen covered rocks that make up these ancient ruined walls have a special charm to them. Their unmovable disposition gives them the esteem of sagacious monks who over eons have become experts in the art of stillness. If they were to speak the numinous wisdom they've absorbed from the wild Earth and the stars throughout their existence, I envisage crowds of thousands of scholars would gather to listen, myself among them.

Breathing deeply, I bring my attention back to the harmonious essence of my botanic companions. Trees are great mentors in stillness, tolerantly enduring the clumsy monkeys who relentlessly grab at and swing across their branches. When I sit with them, I can fully understand what Eckhart Tolle meant when he wrote: *"Look at a tree, a flower, a plant. Let you awareness rest upon it. How still they are, how deeply rooted in being. Allow Nature to teach you stillness."* Trees are quiet and patient, deeply rooted in one spot and slowly stretching to the heavens as they grow over the tens and hundreds and thousands of years of their life span. When one attunes to their tranquil vibrations, they show you how to get comfortable with yourself and to deep practice stillness just as they do. Through their mentoring, I've learnt to accept what is and how to surrender and let go of what no longer serves me. With the act of dropping into stillness and surrendering comes a deepening – in that it's somewhat alchemical magic catalyzes a rush of wildness, a flow of spiritual essence that wells up within the haunted caves of one's heart space flooding it with the blissful presence of radiance, spaciousness, clarity, quietness and wisdom.

A Course in Miracles discusses the idea of the *'Quiet Answer'* in chapter 27. It states:

"In quietness are all things answered, and is every problem quietly resolved."

These words reflect so much truth of the deepening that accompanies extreme stillness. Recondite epiphanies are uncovered in the shades and shadows of a quiet mind. Without the clouded confusion of cluttered thoughts, the path ahead becomes clear and the next step on one's journey is quickly revealed. Allowing myself to sink into the emptiness of a quiet mind and dwell in the presence of a still heart, keeps teaching me to overcome the fear of my unknown wilderness by being present with it. I am made aware that peace abides in the quiet space of my being. When silence befalls the mind, then rays of soul-shine infiltrate the shadowy corners of my unknown wilds. It's a bit like standing on the bank of muddy waters wary of plunging into it for fear of unknown things that may be lurking below the surface, but when all is still, the mud begins to settle and the water sparkles with crystal clarity to reveal the contents beneath. The fear of the unseen threats quickly disappears as all is disclosed in plain sight. Being mindful and aware of the existence your wild unknown territory has a way of demystifying it. Suddenly seeds within are warmed and break into a state of germination. Soon, new life springs forth from the depths of the inner wilderness that was once deemed fallow.

In an article on the historical background of her impressively researched historical book, Lady of the Butterflies, a fictionalized novel about the life of 17th century butterfly enthusiast, author Fiona Mountain highlights that during the period the book was set in it was believed that caterpillars where magically birthed by the leaves of host plants by means of spontaneous generation. In addition, butterflies where thought to be the souls of the dead because of the way they 'entombed' themselves by creating little 'coffins' that the caterpillars went into to undergo some kind of alchemical process and then emerge later as imagines (or adult butterflies). People of the times thought this process was very similar to how humans where buried and placed in coffins when they died. Caterpillars and butterflies where thus the subject of serious superstition. People who were curious about butterflies during those times, where thought to be just as suspicious and were suspected of practicing witchcraft. History is full of examples like this, where a lack of understanding resulted in fear and further preconceived judgments based on those fears. Fortunately, these kinds of suspicions where eventually dispelled by those who took an interest and spent time observing and trying to understand the workings of Nature. Today we know that adult imagines lay their eggs on host plants. Caterpillars hatch from these eggs and after weeks of eating and growing they spin their cocoons, inside which they transform into butterflies. Because we have a clear understanding of what metamorphosis is and how it works, there is nothing frightening about it. The fear of the unknown has been taken out of the equation.

Similarly, by getting up close and personal with your wild unknown – the unfamiliar part of your essence – you soon realize that it was never foreign to you. With each encounter you remember who you really are and you'll find that exploring your unknown wilderness is actually you coming home to yourself. Isn't it a beautiful moment when you come home to yourself? No matter how far you drift from your essence or how long for, the reunion with your wild and beautiful Spirit is precious the moment that you find your way back to your center.

In Stillness Speaks, Eckhart Tolle wrote that by stepping into stillness *'you become present'* and *'you step out of thousands of years of collective human conditioning.'* Along the same vein, Martha Beck wrote that: *'In the silence that comes when your feet leave the earth, you can hear the wild new world calling you to your true nature. The One is whispering to you that what you thought was lost is still yours, that whatever is broken in you can be healed.'* With time and practice, you eventually experience what so many sages preach - that when you are centered in the stillness of the present moment you allow the barriers, beliefs and patterns constructed by the process of domestication to dissolve. Their dissolution gives way to the emergence of a peaceful state of oneness. The more familiar you become with your unknown wilderness, the less elusive it is and the more your curiosity about it grows. Soon, glimpses of tiny cat-like curiosity evolve into a full grown wild lioness-like yearning to inquisitively dive into your inner wilderness with the awakened heart of an explorer in search of new adventures. The journey to the depths of one's soul is a quest so profound. With each new horizon of the inner wilderness that you explore, you feel the expanses of your wild essence growing. To silence your mind and listen to the language of the Divine is to accept a sacred invitation to enter the cave where the unknown wilds have been held captive. It allows you to become a wanderer in the wilderness of your own inner landscapes.

A common fear that I've observed in myself as well as many clients who I worked with while I was doing one-on-one healing sessions is the fear that if you delve into your inner depths, you will discover that you really aren't good enough. Worse, some even fear that they are evil souls who deserve little more than to be punished. It's interesting that many people half expect to discover a monster of sorts at the center of their being. No wonder the idea of entering the cave is daunting. The darkness of the ominous inner caves where your unknown wilds lie hidden may stir a sense of foreboding, as I found in my personal journey. The idea of disturbing creatures lurking in the gloomy cave corners of the soul triggers consternation. For this reason, so many beautiful souls experience resistance on their spiritual journey.

Shekhinah Mountainwater's poem 'Ariadne', which appears in the introductory pages of her book, 'Ariadne's Thread – A Workbook of Goddess Magic' tells the story of how the priestess, Ariadne, guides hero Theseus into a labyrinthine cave in ancient Crete. The myth depicts the labyrinth as a frightening place with a Minotaur at its center (according to Mountainwater this is a patriarchal depiction). Theseus took up the task of liberating Crete from the threat of this monster. In order to do so, he must enter into the labyrinthine cave and conquer the Minotaur. The priestess Ariadne comes to his aid with her magical ball of thread. When Theseus enters the labyrinth, the ball of thread unwinds and rolls along the ground, guiding him all the way to the center where he slays the fearsome Minotaur. On his journey out of the labyrinth, Theseus picks up the magic thread and rewinds it as it guides him back to the entrance safely.

The Minotaur in the spiral cave seems befitting as an analogy for the wild unknown or the parts of your true essence that you've come to fear. The ego and projections of conditioning often convince you that there is one of two ways to deal with your inner wilderness. Either one steers clear of it, or the only other way to handle the perceived danger that it poses is to destroy it. As a result, we find ourselves disconnected from the wild essence, avoiding it at all costs or we strive to tame, break and mold our inner wilds into a placid landscape that adheres to the standards of social conformity.

There is a cave in the midst of the Namibian Kalahari desert called the Dragon's Breath Cave. Like your unknown wilderness, at first glance this dark and dusty cave doesn't exactly appear to be the most welcoming space that one would willingly venture into. Yet it holds a special treasure. About 328 feet (100 meters) down into this cave rests a large pristine underground lake. But that is not all. The underground lake in Dragon's Breath Cave is home to a magnificent rarity – the Golden Cave Catfish. This beautiful golden catfish has been deemed the most isolated and one of the rarest fish in the world. In the same way, what actually resides at the center of your inner wilderness doesn't resemble a monster in any sense of the word. When you journey inward deep into the dark cave, you will find a luminous creature of incredible beauty, patiently waiting to be reacquainted with you. She sits beside the fire, tending to it, keeping it alive. Although, leaving the familiarity of the conventional that we are used to and entering the lair of your unknown wilds can feel so intimidating and unsafe at first, once you do you are bound to unearth rare treasures of insurmountable value. In addition, what was once scary and unknown undergoes yet another metamorphosis and emerges as the full manifestation of yourself – the person who the Divine intended you to be – and that person is so much more than you'd ever imagined.

Re-wilding the spirit reminds me of the chrysalis process of butterflies that I learnt about when I studied a Lepidoptera (the science of butterflies) course. Martha Beck uses a similar analogy in her book, 'Steering by Starlight'. When you journey into the cave that houses unknown aspects of your essence you enter a womb-like space where you undergo a transformation in the same way that a caterpillar enters the pupae and undergoes chrysalis to be transformed into a butterfly. The chrysalis process is messy. The form of what once was becomes a gooey blob when the barriers dissolve. As mentioned, this may leave you in a vulnerable space and give you the sense that your identity has been lost. One of the biggest fears that arise at this point is that misperception that below the surface you are a deeply flawed human being with nothing of value to offer the world. Again, I emphasize that this is completely untrue. So demystifying the uncertainty around your unknown wilderness puts these limiting beliefs and fears to rest. By having a connection with your wild essence, you give yourself a familiar point of reference and sense of self that grounds you through the unshackling process. It gives you greater courage to let go of what was and allow what wants to be and what wants to become to enter.

♥

Practical Ways to Connect with Your Wild Essence

Meditation and mindfulness – Stillness and meditative states are gateways out of the patterns of the mind and into your inner wilderness. With a quiet mind, the negative chatter and limiting beliefs are silenced. Instead, feelings of deep peace arise. Your sense of connection to Divine Spirit is renewed. You see your true essence and your reality more clearly. Threads of wisdom and intuition begin to weave their way into your consciousness. Setting aside some quiet time to meditate for 10 to 30 minutes a day can have a significant healing effect on you. More and more your unknown wilds transform into the wise and comforting luminous essence of your inner self.

Journaling - Journaling is such a simple, yet soothing practice. Through the personal reflection of journaling, you allow your wild essence to find a voice. It's a great way to channel unexpressed feelings, suppressed emotions and to explore your thoughts. It is an avenue through which to explore the different aspects of ourselves, our personality and to observe patterns in our behavior that we may not have been consciously aware of before.

Connecting with your passions – Your passions stem from your wild essence. They are expressions of the physical experiences and things that your soul desires to make manifest. Therefore, connecting with your dreams, passions and desires often puts you in alignment with the vibrations of joy, love and your true self. What excites you? What brings you joy? What are your dreams? Spend time contemplating these things. Create vision boards, spend time doing what you love and devote energy to making your dreams a reality.

♥

These practices are like the ball of thread that Ariadne uses as a guide in and out of the cave. They connect you to your divine feminine intuition or hidden inner knowing. They guide you out of the caves of suppression and into the light of day. The whispers of your wild essence mentioned in Chapter 1 are another thread connecting you to your center. Do you ever hear them? Your wild whispers are ever present reminders seeking you out in big and small ways. Often, they come softly, like kisses in the wind. They were subtle, gentle and mysterious, yet there is something unbridled about them. You hear them calling you to something that you don't fully understand when you mind is still. At times these whispers are so discreet that you almost miss them, other times they are loud and fierce. Your wild whispers are never demanding. Frequently they are the gentle nudges that ask only little things of you. Simple things like, "Love yourself." "Nurture your soul." "Create sacred spaces to invite Spirit in." "Seek the mystery in all things and allow it to fill your heart." "Come out into the garden barefoot after the rain. Feel the damp earth against your soles." One way of liberating your wild essence is to listen for these whispers and follow their directions.

The philosophies shared by *A Course in Miracles* teach that love is a powerful tool that can heal our perceptions of ourselves. I've found a lot of truth in this belief. A valuable lesson that I've learnt during the process of re-wilding my Spirit and demystifying my unknown wilderness is the importance of self-love. The phrase self-love has become common place in the personal development and spirituality arena, so much so that eyes glaze over whenever it comes up because you've seen it and heard it so often. Nonetheless, that doesn't make it any less important and effective in your healing. For a long time, I'd thought of self-love as little things that you do for yourself occasionally. Things like giving yourself a treat, getting a massage, resting when you needed it or saying no to people or things that stress you out. In recent years, my eyes have been opened to the fact that it is something much deeper than that. In the last year in particular while working to heal health issues and overcome the pain of miscarrying my first pregnancy, I began to see that self-love is more about feeling a genuine sense of love and compassion for who I am in every moment. Shortly before that period, I sought out the help of a Kundalini Yoga Healer. As part of the healing program, she shared the relevant mudras and kriyas to assist me, and also briefly introduced me to some of the principles of Kundalini Yoga. I did some additional research on Kundalini principles and found that there are said to be eight stages in the path toward purification of the mind. One of them is called Niyama, which basically refers to the values that you hold for how you treat yourself. This includes values such as purity (having a pure or clean mind and body free of negativity), contentment (being happy with who you are in this moment) and surrender (Let go and let God. Allow yourself to be.) I felt that these niyama values resonated very closely with the concept of self-love. Self-love entails treating yourself with kindness regardless of your perceived flaws, as well as accepting yourself for who you are, including accepting the disowned aspects of yourself – your wild essence - that you may have deserted. Just a little bit of self-love goes a long way. It is a healing balm in any challenge. Creating a sacred space to actively practice a self-love mind-set left me feeling uplifted, renewed and equipped to handle the curve-balls that were thrown my way. Finding ways to love yourself each day can completely transform your life.

I stumbled across a beautiful way of doing this for myself when I was recovering from the aforementioned health issues. My hormones were out of balance, possibly due to a genetic dysfunction with my adrenal glands. I was also diagnosed with Polycystic Ovarian Syndrome. While I was working on healing and finding balance, I felt intuitively guided to turn my bathroom into a sacred space. The voice of my wild essence and Spirit whispered: *'Make your bathroom a Temple of Love.'* I'd not thought about my bathroom that way before, but it made perfect sense as soon as the insight came to me because bathrooms are spaces of self-care where you restore your physical well-being and also replenish your spiritual resources. So for the weeks that followed, my new routine was to enter the *Temple of Love* with consciousness and to bring a new awareness to the space. Regardless of whether it was morning or evening, I'd set aside extra time to be present with myself. I lit candles, indulged in calming essential oils and decided to use some of the gorgeous scented soaps that I'd been saving for a while. I practiced mindfulness with the water, focusing on the feel of it and expressing gratitude for warm water. I visualized the water cleansing my mind, body and soul so that I would be completely renewed. While the bathroom became the *Temple of Love*, I also renamed my bathroom mirror the *'Love Portal'* and made a point of saying 'I love you' along with all my positive affirmations in front of the mirror. I hadn't done mirror work in ages so I'd almost forgotten about how effective it is in creating an inner shift. This is a wonderful way to remind yourself that you are a physical manifestation of Divine love. I tried to see the magic of the Universe in the eyes staring at me in the mirror. Allowing yourself to see the reflection looking back at you in this light can have such a powerful effect on how you see yourself. As a result of these efforts I soon felt the fog of negativity lifting. And I knew that by heeding the guidance of my inner wilderness, my health and well-being was restored bit by bit.

♥

~ **Mantra Moment** ~

(Tweet, Instagram, Share on Facebook
#wildessence #jodiskyrogers)

♥

**"I return to the peace of my wild essence
when I am centered in stillness."**

♥

**"I surrender my fear of the unknown
and embrace my inner wilderness."**

♥

**"I quiet my mind and honor the
Divine intelligence within me."**

♥

**"I find peace and freedom in the
stillness of my wild essence."**

♥

Meditation: Demystify Your Unknown Wilderness

Release the clutter of your conscious mind. Drop into a serene state of oneness.

Visualize a tall wise tree at your center. See its roots growing down your legs, through your feet and reaching deep into the core of the Earth firmly grounding your energy.

The tree at your center is steady, harmonious and silent. Feel the stillness and peace that it radiates. Allow the calming stillness to wash over you. Focus on your wild essence and let the peaceful stillness flow into that part of your being.

Now think about one of the fears or resistances that surfaced when you connected with your inner wilderness in the previous meditation. Be present with what arises. Become aware of any feelings of unease.

Remain mindful of the uneasy feelings that appear. Sense these feelings. Explore them. Stay present with them until the sense of unease dissipates and then surrender them to the well of stillness within.

When the barrier to your wild essence dissolves, allow yourself to spend some time exploring your inner wilderness. Reach below the surface.

What do you discover? What images, feelings or impressions come to mind? How does your wild essence want to be expressed? What does it need to be nurtured?

Listen to its guidance. When you are done, examine healthy ways that you can continue to dissolve your internal resistance and nurture your wild essence.

4

SHEDDING THE SHACKLES

"Surrealism is destructive, but it destroys only what it considers to be shackles limiting our vision."
~ Salvador Dali

Turquoise ocean water shimmers in the sunlight on the West Coast shore, the afternoon sun beating down. My husband and I sit on the soft sand, taking in the salty breeze. My heart is filled with a certain peace seeing him so relaxed. It has been a long year and he has worked so hard. For a few years now, he's seemed jaded and unhappily locked in a soulless job. Fortunately things are changing and new opportunities are opening up to him. This holiday also seems to be bringing his spirit back to life as his wild essence breaks out of confinement. Growing up in the landlocked country of Zimbabwe, coming to the seaside has always been a special treat and somewhat of a spiritual experience for him. Being here has given us both the space to be, to sleep in, to reconnected with one another, enjoy long walks on the beach, spend lazy afternoons reading, to watch the sunset with a glass of Cape wine and most importantly, the space to dream and talk about our heart's deepest desires.

Children laugh loudly playing in the water as they wait for the next big wave to wash in. In front of us, flocks of what seemed like hundreds of darter, a species of aquatic bird, fly southwards over the glistening water. I assume that they must be migrating to mating areas possibly around the estuaries a few miles away. I am mystified by the whole scene. I've never visited this part of South Africa before, and although I've spent much of my life living near the coast in other parts of the country, I've never seen anything like this before either. It's like sweet manna falling from the sky to feed the birdwatcher in me.

A short distance off the shore in the middle of the sea water stands the remains of an abandoned pier. Some of the darters stop to rest on the pier for a little while before they set flight again. I watch as they stretch their long necks and settle into resting position with a statue-like stillness. It's interesting to see how the remnants of this man-made construction torn down by the wear of the ocean and passage of time have now found a new purpose by serving wild Nature. It occurs to me that by breaking down the barriers that you've been taught to build around your wild essence, a powerful ocean of Spirit will reclaim its place in your life, just as the ocean waters wash over a deconstructed pier no longer serving a purpose, to repossess its wild space.

It's funny how we spend our lives walking along the piers of domestication, piers made up of religious rules, politics, careers, houses and the expectations that others have of us, thinking that these piers make up our identity. What a limited view that is to have of oneself. Luckily, we always catch glimpses of light through the cracks in the cement. We see the rush of the ocean through the gaps and it awakens something in us. The big and magnificent truth is that it's not the falsely constructed self that defines us, but rather what lies below, or above or within it – like the vast expanses of wild sea, the seamless blue sky and the golden sand and sun – or in other words, the unlimited spiritual substance of your wild essence. You have the power to abandon those piers of conditioning along with preconceived perceptions of yourself and your life. You are free to choose a different path, one where you can dive deep into a life rich with Spirit, Mystery and the beauty of your wild and true self.

The process of breaking free begins by asking yourself - What stands in the way of me being who I am fully? Whatever it is, how can you release it? How can you walk away from it? Loosen its grips and set your spirit free?

Releasing the Shackles and Reframing Negative Conditioning

I imagine that a snake feels a great deal of liberation when it sheds a skin that has become too tight to accommodate its growing body, as must the grasshoppers and locusts when they molt. What would be of these fascinating creatures if they did not release their restrictive skins/exoskeletons and surrender to the process of becoming who their wild essence is guiding them to become? What becomes of roses' whose sepals fail to part and split to give room for their floral essence to move from bud to bloom? Would they be limited to a sad and short life arrested in development? The Divine spark in each of us is designed to grow with expansive freedom and blossom in wild abandon. But fulfilling this inspired destiny means to cast aside the heavy weights of suppression and to dispose of the shackles of confinement. To release the shackles of domestication, it is helpful to understand how they manifest in your life. Depending on our experiences, each of us has picked up different beliefs and patterns which have been shaped by our conditioning.

The subject of conditioning brings two stories to mind. The first relates to a poignant moment in my life. In my early childhood in the early eighties, I found myself on the wrong side of the color and race line of the racist South African apartheid regime. The apartheid system was abolished and Nelson Mandela was released when I was eight years old. At the age of 12, I witnessed the first democratic election and the exciting and relatively peaceful transformation of my country into a new democracy and suddenly we became a land of possibilities. The gate to a world of opportunities that were previously denied to my oppressed parents, grandparents and predecessors because of their skin color was now suddenly open. A couple of years later, I was in a classroom full of my fellow classmates and three Youth Outreach Officers. They worked for a Christian non-governmental organization and came to our school occasionally to give life skills training.

The topic for discussion on that particular day was 'internal oppression'. One of the Youth workers listed the various racial groupings in a random fashion on the chalk board at the front of the classroom. He then asked the class to arrange the different race groupings in order of importance or superiority. I was taken aback by his request, but was even more shocked to that my fellow classmates began arranging the words written on the chalk board in order of perceived superiority mutually agreeing that it was right to placing white people at the top of the list and black people at the very bottom. I was a shy child so I stayed quiet for a long time, but it infuriated me to the point that I couldn't contain my anger anymore and very rudely shouted out to the Youth worker. I don't recall my exact words, but what I said was something along the lines of:

"Who gives anyone the right to decide that some people are more superior or more deserving than others? It's racist and judgmental. It is sad that some people think so much or so little of themselves that they fail to see that we are all equal."

One of the other students answered: *"But that's what we were taught,"* and didn't seem to understand what I was upset about.

Caught up in my fury of anger, I was completely disarmed when the Youth worker responded:

"Exactly!"

I sheepishly realized that that was exactly the point they were trying to make with this exercise. They were demonstrating to us that even though we no longer lived under the oppressive apartheid rule, many of us were still internally oppressed and where conditioned to believe that we were inferior. This conditioning translated into self-limiting beliefs that deeply affected people's perceptions of themselves and took away their personal power. These were the internal scars that our nation's people were still grappling with. Being brought to this realization was a notable moment in my life. It hit home that often we are taught to believe things or act in certain ways, but that doesn't always make them true or right. It would have been rather sad if so many people continued to live shackled with the belief that they were inferior and incapable of creating better lives for themselves just because of their race. We need to question things and decide for ourselves whether or not they diminish and limit us or whether they liberate and empower us. South Africa has made so much progress over the last two decades, and although there is still so much more that needs to be done to rectify imbalances and to empower the impoverished, every day I am inspired and feel privileged to see how South Africans break through molds and release their oppressive mindsets to build communities, chase their dreams and create miracles. Examples of people overcoming similar experiences can be found in numerous places around the world. We gain great value from heeding lessons from them.

The second story, which is a completely different example, but just as significant because it is a clear demonstration of the impact of conditioning, comes from a woman that I once met. For the purpose of this story I'll call this acquaintance Monica. Monica had difficulty interacting with others and fitting into different social settings. When her new boyfriend invited her to a social gathering to meet his friends for the first time, Monica was overcome with extreme anxiety. The day of the occasion eventually arrived and Monica went to the gathering with her boyfriend. As soon as they got there she immediately felt uncomfortable with the way everyone was looking at her. She felt that they were asking probing questions because they did not like her or thought that she wasn't good enough for their friend. Feeling that she was under attack, Monica began to act out by drinking heavily, barking at anyone who asked her questions about her interests or her life and making disparaging remarks about people's clothes or the way that they looked. Whenever her boyfriend was in conversation with one of his female friends, she would rudely interrupt their conversation in an attempt to draw his attention back to her. Needless to say, her new boyfriend and his friends were not impressed by her behavior. In the car ride on the way home, Monica screamed at her boyfriend for not defending her when his friends were judgmental and attacking. She also accused him of flirting with his female friends. Her boyfriend was taken aback by her reaction. He said that from his perspective, he felt that his friends were very excited to meet her. They were not judging or attacking her, but merely trying to get to know her. He was embarrassed by her heavy drinking and felt that she was extremely rude, judgmental and irrational. He was also very insulted by her accusations about flirting with his friends. The next day, he ended their relationship and said that he was not interested in seeing her again. She was crushed to face the failure of yet another relationship.

Monica added that when she sobered up and had time to think about what had happened she realized that her behavior was indeed out of line. While discussing the incident with Monica, she said that she was so afraid that her boyfriend would dump her and that was exactly what happened. Upon further dissecting the underlying negative beliefs that motivated her behavior, I found Monica had a difficult childhood. She came from a broken home and received very little affection or consideration from either of her parents. She was exposed to a lot of abuse and harsh treatment. As a result of her upbringing, she developed several self-limiting beliefs. Every day she would tell herself: *"I am not good enough." "No one will ever love me." "People always judge me."*

Consequently, these underlying beliefs fueled her insecurities and perceptions of various situations. When she felt threatened, she would act out. Because she felt people were judging her, she was subconsciously behaving in a way that would inevitably attract the very things that she wanted to avoid, thus creating a self-fulfilling prophecy. In the end, she was so busy living out the script of her negative beliefs, that her wild essence remained hidden. After doing some self-examination and going for several life coaching and therapy sessions, Monica was finally able to get to the root of her problems. Once she understood her underlying beliefs and how they affected her, she was able to start deconstructing them and releasing them.

Monica's story is an extreme example of the impact that negative conditioning has on you. Fortunately, it doesn't have to stay that way. Like Monica, once you dig a little below the surface, you can find ways to start undoing these beliefs and replacing them with more positive ones that allow you to grow and expand.

How do limiting beliefs surface in your life? How do they affect you? What are the negative things that you believe and tell yourself every day? Spend a few days observing your thoughts. Note your reactions to situations and how you approach different experiences. Is there anything in particular that triggers your negative beliefs? Each time you become aware of a limiting or negative thought, note it down.

Write down one or two self-limiting beliefs or negative thoughts that came up for you:

_____
_____
_____
_____
_____
_____

Once you've identified your shackles, you'll then be able to start loosening their grips by deconstructing and reframing these beliefs. One way of doing that is to dispel the belief by finding one or two reasons why it is not true. When you live with a belief for a long time, it becomes so engrained that you believe it's completely true. So by presenting the egoic mind with evidence that the belief is unfounded, you make it easier to release these negative perceptions from your consciousness.

Take the first limiting belief that you've identified in the exercise above. Now find one or two reasons why the negative belief is not true:

_____

_____

_____

_____

_____

_____

Shifting Your Perspective

The lenses through which we view our lives greatly affect the situations that we attract. Along my journey, I discovered that it's not been about healing the fractured parts of myself, but rather healing my perception of myself, as well as my perception of the world. This has meant learning to see myself and the situations around me through the compassionate eyes of my own heart.

I have a birthmark on my head - A patch of translucent pale skin that stretches across my temple on the right side of my face. The patch of hair around my birthmark grows out blonde, a stark contrast to the rest of my mousy brown hair. As a child, I was often teased because of it. Other kids called me all sorts of hurtful names and often told me that I was an ugly freak. And that was how I felt – like an ugly freak. Their reactions to my birthmark convinced me that I was deeply flawed and worthless. Then one day when I was about 8 or 9 years old, one of my aunts was visiting for a few days. Somehow the topic of my birthmark came up in conversation and she mentioned that she thought it was beautiful. My immediate response was: *"No, it's not!"* I responded immediately. *"Everyone says it's ugly."*

What she said next completely changed the way that I thought about myself. My aunt told me that the next time someone tormented me about it I should just tell them that I have a birthmark because I was *'touched by God'*. I don't think she realized what a profound affect her words had on me. The idea that my birthmark was not a flaw but a reminder of being touched by the loving hand of something Sacred made me feel so special. Suddenly, the unkind insults didn't hurt so much anymore and I began to see myself and my destiny in a different light. It just took that single moment of clarity to shift my negative perception of myself. Shifting from a limiting perspective to one that is expansive is thus a powerful way of releasing the subjugative shackles.

Again, *A Course in Miracles'* principles which attribute healing to shifting from a place of fear to a place of love comes to mind. Author and spiritual teacher, Gabrielle Bernstein, often communicates that this entails being willing to witness your fears and limiting beliefs, surrendering them to what she calls your inner guide, or in other words the wisdom of your wild essence and then shifting to a perspective centered in love instead.

Unlike the limiting ego-based self, your intuitive wild essence is always grounded in truth and has a clear idea of how to create situations that help you to tap into your unlimited potential. It allows the incredible beauty inside of you to gleam with radiance. I recently came across a research paper published with the 'Applied Animal Behavior Science Journal' in March 2013 that described how a group of Hungarian scientists investigated the difference in behavioral responses between hand-reared wolves and tamed dogs. During the study, both the wolves and dogs were tied to trees. They were allowed some freedom of movement, but could not break free. For one part of the study, the wolves and dogs were approached by a person first in a friendly manner, and then in an aggressive manner. The results of the study showed something very interesting. When the dogs were approached, they monitored the human's behavior very closely. They responded in a playful manner to the person's friendliness, but when they were approached aggressively they retaliated with aggression showing that they felt threatened. On the other hand, while most of the wolves also responded to friendliness, they did not react to the being approached by a person aggressively. The wolves seemed to understand that no real threat was being posed to them.

Similarly, when someone allows themself to fall into the entrapments of limiting and negative thought systems, they live from a place of fear and often react strongly to harmless external situations. This is because these situations make them feel threatened in a similar way to how the tamed dogs felt. When they find themselves in situations that trigger negative inner dialogue, they become defensive, self-critical and judgmental of both themselves and of others as we saw in Monica's case. Sometimes what is required is to relinquish the control of the ego-based self by turning things over to your wild essence. Like the wolves, your wild essence is able to make more sound assessments of the situations that you find yourself in. Your wild essence chooses not to react but rather to walk the road of peace which is brightly lit by the luminous glow of love, dreams and spiritual growth. Just making small internal shifts like this can translate into miraculous changes in your outer experiences.

So how can you shift your perceptions when you are caught in a sticky spot that triggers a negative mindset?

One quiet afternoon on the beach, I sat on the fine white sand of the shore. The breeze was warm and comforting, despite the grey cloudy sky overhead. I was sure that a vicious storm was just hours away. The ocean took on the same grey color and the horizon melted away as sea and sky seamlessly flowed into one. Seagulls walked the shore, stalking sand crabs as they scurried around. Looking at them running sideways made me wonder what it must be like to see the world from that viewpoint. I made a short note of my musings in my nature journal and later stuck a picture of a crab next to what I'd written. The next day, I found myself wondering if perhaps the crabs that I'd encountered on the beach had an animal spirit message for me. So I did some research to find out what the crab spirit teaches. I discovered that crabs are connected to the watery Goddess and lunar cycles and often represent feminine cycles, rebirth and trust. But not surprisingly, they also call us to shift to different perspectives and view the situations that we face or life in general from another angle. Since then, it made me view the process of shifting perspective as getting into **'the crab mindset'.** I've had a lot of fun using the technique to shift my focus in a more positive direction.

The crab mindset technique is simple and quick. Here is how it works:

1. *When a negative or self-limiting belief surfaces stop for a moment and focus on it.*
2. *Analyze the thought. Where does it come from? Does it stem from a place of fear, anger or hurt? What triggered it?*
3. *Now take a deep breath. Step into the crab mind mode. Allow yourself to view life from a different perspective. Flip this belief on its head by viewing yourself or your situation from a place of loving compassion.*
4. *Centered in this place of love, create a new belief or thought that is compassionate, nurturing, inspiring and expansive.*

To explain a bit further, let's say that you really want to become an author and write inspiring books. But, whenever you find yourself connected to the flow of your wild essence or you feel inspired by this precious dream and imagine how incredible it would be to be a published author, the limiting voice of conditioning pops up and reminds you that you are dyslexic. At the back of your mind you hear the internalized voices of your parents, siblings or teachers saying:

"You can't read or string a descent sentence together. You'll never be an author."

This thought triggers pain, brings fears to the surface and leaves you disappointedly feeling that your dream is not possible.

Then when you take a moment to breathe, be present and shift into the crab mindset you enter into a completely different mind space – one filled with love and compassion for yourself. This is a mind space full of endless possibilities. You give yourself permission to release this limiting belief. Now you invite your wild essence to dream up a new encouraging and supportive belief to replace the negative one. You listen for the wild whispers, until you witness a new thought forming. Perhaps it is something like: *"You can do anything that you put your mind to, regardless of the challenges that you face"*….or *"You are an inspiring writer and author with so many beautiful and uplifting stories to share."*

Forgiveness

"The wound is the place where light enters you." ~ Rumi

Yesterday, I saw a friend's status update on one of the social media platforms that said: *"Forgiveness is overrated."* While I could somewhat understand what could make her feel that way, I feel that it couldn't be further from the truth. The power of forgiveness surfaced a lot when I was in the process of shedding my own shackles. In many instances, it has been the most difficult exercise for me to do. When you are releasing, breaking down blocks and analyzing the root of limiting beliefs or negative behavioral patterns, you inevitably unearth several traumatic experiences, memories and past hurts. It becomes very tempting to want to hold on to these things and to project a lot of anger onto those who have wronged you in the past - parents who put themselves first and neglected their parental duties, teachers who crushed your spirit, lovers who broke your heart and all of the abusers or tormentors who showed up in your life in different masks. Shedding has a way of opening up these deep wounds. It is worth noting that if these wounds are not soothed and carefully nursed to healing, they will merely fester and ooze out more bitter negativity that will trickling out into your life. Un-forgiveness is a terrible burden to carry because you find yourself reliving difficult experiences over and over again. The resentment and anger keep you stuck in the past just as much as the other person involved in the situation. It also becomes a barrier that shuts out your wild essence.

Forgiving, healing and releasing the past is thus just as important as consciously releasing the negative mindset that keeps you caged in a spaces that don't resonate with your true essence. This is not to deny the weight of the pain that you experience as a result of the past. Nor is it to say that the hurtful or abusive behavior should be excused or tolerated. But forgiveness is part of the process of acknowledging that you have survived the past and are giving yourself permission to move forward and feel whole again in spite of it. It means allowing your wild essence to soar despite the people or challenges that have endeavored to demean you, whether they did so consciously or unconsciously.

There are two realities that I've had to come to terms with in dealing with my own past, when healing hurt and learning to forgive. The first is that the person or people who have hurt you are acting out their own reality in the best way that they know how. When you look deeper into their stories and their histories, you are bound to find that they have been conditioned in a negative manner. More often than not, abusers have been abused themselves. People who are bad parents are likely to have been neglected or ill-treated by their own parents. A partner who uses you and is afraid to commit to your relationship has probably been hurt or cheated on in the past. In her book, You Can Heal Your Life, inspirational author Louise Hay says that part of forgiveness means accepting that we are all doing the best that we can and understanding that the people who hurt you didn't know any better. Louise Hay's book has an incredible meditation on forgiveness. This meditation entails visualizing the person that you need to forgive as a child who is probably frightened or feeling hurt themselves, and then seeing that child getting the love, attention and all that they need to nurture their little souls. Activities like Louise Hay's beautiful meditation are an effective tool that can help you understand their behavior better and to let the past go.

The other reality is that, as much as I've wanted to stay angry about certain things in my past, all of my experiences, both good and bad have made me who I am today. I once read that storms make tree roots grow deeper. The wild essence has a similar response to the trials that you face. We are adaptable creatures. Challenges help your spirit to grow. Each occasion you face testing times, then the harsh voices of self-doubt, criticism and fear may pipe up to reduce you. Yet, regardless of how loud these voices shout, there is a little spark of wilderness in you that remembers the vast strength and magic of your wild essence. That spark, a tiny and a dim flint, sets a wild fire alight in your heart. Although you are not fully cognizant of it at the time, it's the part of you that remembers the Divine plans that the Universe is carving out with your soul. Your wild essence is the part of you that carries on even when you are questioning *why* you are carrying on or what you have to live for. It is the part of you that knows something waits on the other side of tomorrow, something called destiny. In the midst of your trials and chaos, sometimes you do stumble into still moments where you connect with your wild essence. When that happens, a sense of calm befalls you and pieces of the big picture are put into context.

When I reflect, I always find that there was something valuable that I learnt from my experiences. My trials have shaped me, built my character and deepened my understanding of myself and of life. I frequently see that had I not faced a certain difficulty, I would not have gained the insights that have influenced my life and others positively later on. Had I not struggled with emotional challenges, abuse and bullying as a child then perhaps I would not have discovered the enriching and deeply spiritual path that I am on now. My need to escape toxic situations and the wrath of abusive personalities drove me to seek out the peace of Nature where I developed a profound spiritual connection with the wild Earth. My experiences of being bullied, harassed and rejected for being different deepened my empathy and allowed me to release my judgments of others. My battle with depression and suffering helped me to understand the suffering of others. It set me on a path to heal myself and inspired me to want to heal, uplift and inspire others as well. I believe that your experiences, regardless of how dreadful they may be to live through, are always preparing you to play the part of the ultimate role that you're destined to embody, the role of your magnificent wild essence.

Taking this into cognizance and finding a way to focus on the indirect treasures that came out of your tragic experiences could help you to see forgiveness differently.

Wild Earth as a Mentor

I love witnessing the bravery that the first flowers of the new season demonstrate when they open their little petals and fill my garden with sweet scents weeks before winter came to a close. It must take a certain trust in the unseen forces of the Divine to courageously awaken from the bud state and blossom. These gentle creatures teach us the delicate art of opening up and confidently sharing extraordinary gifts with the world. They blossom fearlessly and are a mirror of the love and beauty alive within each of us.

When I was coming to terms with having a miscarriage a few short weeks after the joy of discovering that I was pregnant, I felt that Great Mother Earth was kind to me. In her gentle manner, she taught me about the secret life of surrender. Her lessons come in the quiet Fall whispers of the falling leaves, shedding bark and in the way that fluffy feather-like seeds float through the air. It is difficult to explain, but these simple things soothed my and showed me how to accept what was, how to surrender my pain and to flow with the process of healing. It's easy to hold on to a well of negative emotions and to remain stuck in a dark spell. It is easy to want to battle with what can't be undone and to try and control what is out of our hands. Surrender always feels like the harder job. But during those Fall mornings when I didn't want to face life, the sound of the howling wind drew me out of bed.

Letting go and giving myself over to the hands of the Divine, the Goddess, the Earth, I found my way to a state of wild grace. In moments when I felt most deserted and let down, I felt held in sacredness. It was comforting. I discovered that even when I felt that I didn't always know how to carry on, I just needed to allow it to guide me and to heal me until I returned to restoration. During that period, the Earth became a wise and understanding teacher. I learnt that she too had lost children – Stillborn seeds that sprouted roots but then never lived to see the light of day. Forests and meadows cleared and devastated by destruction. Animals hunted for sport. She showed me how to move forward, slowly and gracefully. The wild Earth guided me through the seasons despair, anger and grief, showing me how to pass through it on step at a time. Nature has been an ever present reminder of how to keep breathing. I learnt that although the world doesn't stop for pain, sometimes we just need to stop and rest for a while as life carries on. Sometimes quiet moments sitting on the grass and watching the bees float from flower to flower just as they always do is constant enough to bring a touch of stability to a world that is crumbling from grief.

Wild Earth is a story of hope. She turns endings into new beginnings. New life always returns to places that have been ravaged by violent fires. At winter's end the Crocus and Lily of the valley push their pretty little heads through the snow. Even arid deserts hold wild stories of hope and promise. The Earth shows us how to start over. Most important of all, every day she shows me that the same strength, resilience and light abide inside of me.

♥

Animals reared in captivity or kept captive for prolonged periods have trouble adjusting to the wild. It takes time to slowly reintegrate them into the wilderness. Likewise, if you've spent a long time succumbing to the mental and psychological subjugation of conditioning, then adjusting to the freedom of a life centered in your wild essence may take some getting used to. You may become fearful of not knowing how to be or how to express your true essence because you are simply not used to it.

"The human spirit needs places where Nature has not been rearranged by the hand of man."
~ Author Unknown

It is worth bearing in mind that wild Earth can be a mentor in your process of reclaiming your inner wilderness. I've experienced this first hand throughout my life. Nature mirrors your wild essence and all of the luminous intelligence that your existence carries. Spending time in the wild and Nature spaces allows you to absorb the Great Mother's wisdom and soulful lessons. By tapping into the vibration of wild Earth, the resonance of your wild essence amplifies. The Earth is laden with lessons and metaphors that can offer guidance and teach you how to release shackles and live immersed in the peace and freedom of your natural self. This is why connecting with Nature is a key part of the activities that I outline for participants of my Spirit Wilding e-Course. It is hugely beneficial to find a Nature space that you can connect with while working to release the effects of conditioning. Not only does Nature teach you about your own wildness, it also helps you to relax. Spending time in the natural world grounds you and raises your energetic vibration. Having a deep relationship with the Earth means that you also benefit by drawing on the nurturing, abundant and loving energy of this Great Mother, making you feel supported on your journey. That way you feel connected to life, the Earth and the Universe and are aware that you are never alone.

Overcome the Fear of Returning to Your Wild Essence

The Safari van came to a halt. Our tour guide motioned to the tall dry grasses on the right. We peered out of the side of the van at the sea of dusty yellow grass searching for signs of life, but there were none. Then suddenly the lion lifted its head from the grass and yawned. He was a strapping adult male with a thick golden mane. We'd been on his trail for almost an hour now. Excitement and fear danced together in my chest, as I watched in awe. It doesn't matter how many times you've seen it, there is something incredible about seeing these predators in the wild. He sat perfectly poised starring contently out ahead, as if taking in the crimson sunset. The guide driving the Safari van decided to drive closer to the lion so that we could get a better look at him and to allow the members of our party to take pictures of the magnificent king of the African wild. Only, that meant leaving the side of the Safari van where my husband and I were sitting completely open in full view of the lion. Being exposed in this way left me feeling anxious and vulnerable. In a swift movement the lion stood up to reveal the rest of his body and golden fur. It startled me. More and more I realized that less than 5 meters away from me lies real danger. He walked a few paces and sat down in the long grass again, leaving only his head in sight once more. My companions around me were excitedly clicking their cameras and getting as many pictures of the beast as possible. Suddenly, the lion twisted his head in dismay and I swear he stared directly at me. His eyes were fierce and piercing. My heart stopped as a wave of fear washed over me. In my mind's eye, I could already see him charging at us and sinking his teeth into my limbs. That became a real possibility. Something had upset him. The tour guide whispered *"Stop clicking, stop clicking!"* motioned for everyone to stop taking pictures. The sound of the clicking cameras seemed to be irritating the lion. Dead silence descended over the Safari van as everyone held their breath. All that I heard was the sounds of the bush around me. In that moment, it hit home that being so close to a lion was a risky situation warranting real fear. All of my ego-based fears and limiting beliefs no longer mattered. The fear of connecting to my own essence and giving myself permission to be who I was, seemed like ridiculous stories in the face of real fear. Something about the experience put so much into perspective. After a while the lion stood up again and looked longingly at the horizon. He slowly strolled away. The tour guide mentioned that he was probably going to join up with the lionesses on the other side of the game reserve. We watched as the daylight continued to fade and he disappeared into the distance.

Shamans and medicine women and men of various indigenous cultures around the world view big cats as spirit messengers. The teachings of these feline predators involve overcoming fears and finding the courage to make leaps of faith. When I did my Munay Ki training to learn and become a teacher of this Peruvian shamanic system, one of the five archetypal animals that we connected with was Otoronogo which is the sister jaguar/puma/panther archetype. In my training I worked on integrating Otorongo energy to release fears that held me back from pursuing my life purpose and path as a spiritual teacher/healer, as well as to cultivate the courage to make the necessary life changes to support my path. Master Life Coach and author, Martha Beck, reinforces the symbolic role of feline predators in conquering fear in her book, 'Finding You Way in a Wild New World', when she describes a recurring dream that she had about being attacked by a leopard. Upon looking deeper into the meaning of the dream, Beck discovered that some shamans, or menders as she calls them, have dreams of being devoured by wild cats early in their journey and that this is seen as a call to release the old domesticated self to walk a path steered by Spirit. Their initial instinct is for their dream self to resist being killed by the leopard or jaguar or whichever wild cat they encounter. However, it is when the shaman lets go of their fear of this beast and surrenders to the attack that they experience the transformation that liberates the wild essence. At this point the recurring dream stops.

Fear manifests in so many ways. Breaking through the restrictions of domestication and witnessing the emergence of your wild self will stir up a whirlwind of underlying fears. You may be afraid of how others will perceive you or judge you as you make the life changes that your soul desires. You may be afraid of the sound of your wild whispers and the things that this voice asks you to do for yourself. Sometimes that inner voice asks you to step out of you comfort zone and do bold things. It will call you to shine your brilliant light even though you feel safe hiding in the shadows. Becoming aware of your inner world may scare you and make you uncomfortable to be present with yourself. Perhaps just looking deep into your own eyes in the mirror and seeing the expansive depths that lies within you is scary. Because you have faced many experiences that have negatively influenced your self-image and have tried to diminish your Spirit, stepping into your own power may feel unfamiliar and terrifying. Questions like *'Who am I to be wild and bold?"* may echo at the back of your mind. As Marianne Williamson's renowned quote puts it – *"who are you not to?"* When fear arises, sometimes you need to allow yourself to feel the fear and be who you are or do what needs to be done anyway. You are here for a reason and your wild essence was created to be expressed. Remind yourself that when facing moments of fear are always opportunities to transmute it and to turn it over to a place of loving light. Just as wounds are a place where light enters according to mystic poet Rumi, let your moments of fear be an entrance for the light of Divine Spirit to illuminate a pathway to your wild essence.

On the other end of the spectrum there is a different kind of fear – the fear that you have been disconnected from your true essence for so long, perhaps it no long exists. You may battle to hear your inner whispers and see no signs of life each time you check the pulse of your wild self. This triggers the fear that you might find a hollow shell should you dig below the surface. Again, like Mother Nature, the wild essence is resilient. Like seeds that have been frozen in permafrost for 3,000 years, once it has had a little time to thaw, it can be germinated and reawakened to new life. Keep sending little nudges its way. Moments of stillness watching the clouds float by. Walking barefoot on the grass. Gazing up at the stars and howling to the full moon. Little things that make you giggle and that fill your heart with joy. Keep releasing the things that break you down or reduce your sense of self. Keep nurturing yourself however you can, and bit by bit that inner wilderness will begin to thrive again. It may be slow, but it will happen at the pace that it needs to happen at.

When You Stumble

The process of un-shackling doesn't happen overnight. Although it gets easier with time, it does require continuous effort to strip away the things that cage your essence layer by layer. I've stumbled a lot along the way. Chances are that you will too. And it is okay because this is a natural part of the process. It is a normal part of life in general. Coming face to face with your negative inner dialogue and limiting beliefs, one can see quite clearly how easy it is for you to be your own worst enemy. It is vital that you learn to be your own best friend. When you meet stumbling blocks in your path, it is tempting to resort back to being self-critical and beat yourself up about it. But that is exactly when you need to be most supportive and compassionate with yourself. Celebrate each little bit of progress that you do make instead of focusing too much on the things that you do wrong. Forgive yourself for your mistakes. You are doing the best that you can just as we all are. Take in the lessons that the situation is teaching you and then get on with it. I always draw inspiration from the male weaver birds and how they persevere when it comes to building their nests. Masters at their nest building art, they weave together grass, leaves and flowers to build their little kingdoms. They build one nest after the other, always expanding their families. When females are not attracted to a newly build nest, they immediately get to work tearing it down and rebuilding another one. Remember to be patient with yourself and keep putting one foot in front of the next. In time when you look back, you will be amazed at how far you have come.

♥

~ Mantra Moment ~

(Tweet, Instagram, Share on Facebook
#wildessence #jodiskyrogers)

♥

**"I release the limiting thoughts that keep
me locked in negative patterns."**

♥

**"The barriers to my wild essence
dissolve in the peace of stillness."**

♥

**"The more I let go of my internal blocks, the more I
experience the peace and freedom of my wild essence."**

♥

**"I allow the wise loving light of my wild
essence to illuminate my path."**

♥

Meditation: Release Your Barriers and Fears

You will need a pen, a piece of paper and a flower or two
for this meditation exercise. Once you have them, find a
peaceful spot in Nature, a place in your garden, at a park,
in a forest or near a lake, whichever suites you best.

Ensure that you will not be disturbed. Sit down comfortably.
Close your eyes. Breathe in and out slowly as you relax and
center yourself. Connect to the peaceful energy of your wild
essence for a few moments.

Then visualize roots growing down from that space and connecting with the energy body of the Earth. Feel the loving and supportive energy of the Earth rising into your body and grounding you.

Set the intention to release your fears and barriers that reduce your wild essence or keep you stuck in negative patterns. On your piece of paper, write down a list of fears, restrictive thoughts and self-limiting beliefs that you would like to release from your life.

Now pick up your flower. Look at your list, focus on releasing the first item on it as you pick a petal and let it go. As you do, say: *"I no longer need this. I release it to Mother Earth to be transformed from fear to love."*

Visualize Mother Earth taking your fear, or self-limiting belief and transmuting it into a positive flow of loving energy.

Repeat this with each item on your list.

Notice how you feel as you release each item. Are you letting go completely? Is there a part of you that is holding on to negativity? If so keep doing the exercise and visualizing the block leaving you until you feel that you are free of it.

Focus on the feeling of freedom expanding in you as you release your barriers and blocks. Be present with the feeling of lightness as your wild essence grows. Ask the Divine intelligence of your inner wilderness for further guidance on how to release fears and blocks even more. Listen for the answers your intuition shares. Are you guided to go for therapy or additional healing to release the grips of conditioning? Does your inner essence want you to de-clutter you home or work environment to release stagnant energy? Do you need to do a dietary detox? How can you follow through to take the right steps for your highest good?

When you are ready to end the meditation, take the list, tear it up and dispose of it in a safe manner. This helps to symbolically release it from your consciousness.

Unearth Your
Wild Treasures

"We gather up the lost pieces of ourselves and slowly, with great love and intention, begin the work of re-membering our spirits, our flesh, and the way we desire to live our lives."
~ Hillary Rain and Denise Andrade-Kroon

It was a warm late summer evening. Grandmother moon glowed in fullness, stamping the night sky with a circle of light as her silver reflection danced on the water. Walking on the sea sand with my amphibious sneakers felt so strange considering that I was used to feeling my bare feet in the shifting sand. A group of us had gathered for an educational Nighttime Beach Tour to view the sea life that had made their home in the rock pools along the shore. The full moon meant a high tide and a greater chance of aquatic life activity. Climbing over the rocks and wading through the swallow pools with nothing more than a few torch lights in the dark, was unnerving at first. But once our eyes adjusted and we began looking closely, shining our torches into the dark corners of the rock pools we discovered some fascinating treasures. Excitement filled the air, people 'ooh-ing' and 'ah-ing' as we moved about spotting urchins, sea cucumbers, starfish, crabs, several species of octopi and interesting looking fish hidden in mysterious places. I'd often spent time exploring rock pools during the day and never had I come across so much vibrant sea life. It was an exhilarating experience. I live for moments like that, ones where life presents us with all kinds of surprises, precious gifts and treasures when we look in the right places. It reminds me of one of the moment in my childhood when my grandfather took my cousin and I for a walk along the river to one of the nearby waterfalls. There were clusters of smoothed boulders at the foot of the falls. While I was walking on one of the boulders, I noticed a few puddles on its surface. I put my bare foot into one puddle. The water was cool against my skin. I examined the odd shape of the puddle outline. Then it hit me that what I was looking at appeared to be very much like a dinosaurs footprint.

"Grandpa!" "Grandpa!" I shouted in excitement. *"The dinosaurs where here! Look at their footprints."*

My grandfather turned to look and then laughed.

"Those aren't dinosaur footprints, they are just puddles carved into the rock by years of water erosion," he responded.

Alas, his words where lost on me. To my wildly imaginative five year old mind, I had discovered the fossilized paw prints of a mysterious dinosaur and no one was going to convince me otherwise. I bent down and put my hand into the puddle to touch the bottom of it, pressing my palm against the spot where I whole-heartedly believed that a dinosaur once stood. In that brief moment, I'd uncovered a great treasure. There have been many such moments in my life. Whether stumbling upon dinosaur footprints or seeking out elusive aquatic creatures, these dear experiences remind me that there are treasures hidden in the landscapes of our inner wilderness too. This is because the more acquainted you become with you wild essence and unshackle, the more likely you are to unearth the diamonds, emeralds and rubies resting in your heart. When the voices of doubt are laid to rest and the cage door is opened, you will experience your wild soul emerging in ways that you never thought possible. Precious dreams that have long been buried will find their way back into your conscious space. You may rediscover your gifts, your talents that have long been suppressed, never having the space to flourish. You may uncover new found strengths and virtues within yourself that so many negative voices told you, you don't have.

Early in 2014, when I visited my parents, they gave me an antique book called Gold Dust, a collection of devotionals and insights from French monks that was published in 1880. Growing up, I was charmed by its antiquity. As it turned out, the contents were just as inspiring. I remember running my fingers over the intricate details of the embossed midnight blue cover and tracing the letters of the gold imprinted title, before opening the book to a random page to read what spiritual wisdom the pages had to offer. So I was delighted to receive this gift both for its sentimental value and for my love of collecting out of print books. To give the reader an understanding of the origins of the title, the introduction of Gold Dust explains that at one point in the old days, young children and the old and infirm poor in the South of France who were unable to work would search the dry beds of rivers for 'golden dust which sparkles in the sun' (Paillettes d'Or). While gold dust was not as valuable as giant nuggets of solid gold, nor did it hold the stature of precious gemstones, it was a great treasure to these people because collecting and selling it gave them a source of income for food and some semblance of a livelihood. It gave them hope to get through their hardships. The passage in the introduction goes further to say: *"What is done by these poor people and little children for the gold dust God has sown in those obscure rivers, we would do with those counsels and teachings which God has sown almost everywhere, which sparkle, enlighten, and inspire for a moment, then disappear, leaving but regret that the thought did not occur to collect and treasure them."*

To the monks who compiled the book of devotions, their spiritual insights and moments of inspiration were their golden dust, their treasures. The hidden riches of your soul are yours. The treasures that you unearth at the core of your wild essence will look different to what someone else's does. But regardless of the form that they take in your life, when you remove the barriers that have kept you from your center and learn to live in union with your inner wilderness you will certainly witness how the magic of the Universe comes alive in you.

"I must be a mermaid. I have no fear of depths." ~ Anais Nin

Having entered the cave of your unknown inner wilderness to see it transformed into a beautiful unrestricted place of magic, a peaceful retreat, you eventually become comfortable enough with your true essence to explore it in deeper ways. Exploring your spiraling cave, you start to notice things that you may not have seen before. You essentially become like a spiritual paleontologist who uncovers obscure fossils in the cave floor, fossils that tell the tale and history of your soul. Perchance, you may happen across a dusty old suitcase in one of the cave corners where your old mermaid tail is kept. Swimming with this tail brings about an alchemical reaction that allows you to breathe underwater. So from time you time, you'll feel brave enough you put it on and dive deeper into the underground lake of your cave than you ever have before. There you are blessed with the opportunity to swim with your proverbial Golden catfish, reveling at how this enchanting creature shimmers as it sleekly glides through the water. In the depths of the underground lake, what will you discover? Perhaps you'll be lucky enough to discern even more new treasures, aspects of your wild self that are ready to be returned to you. Through the eyes of a spiritual paleontologist you also start to notice things like the paint markings on the cave walls. They are guide posts left by the ancients who were there before you. Looking closer you will find that some of these rock paintings look remarkably like your own creations. They are made up of your colors and your brush strokes, nuances of your hand prints and they even hold traces of your scent. This is because they are yours. They are traces of yourself that you left behind as reminders that you have been here before. Left as a touch of familiarity to rekindle your memory of your wild self and to draw to your awareness the fact that you are not charting the dark and scary shadow lands of the inner wilds, but merely coming home to a place that you're already acquainted with.

"Her stone carvings express her mystical knowledge, her healing repertoire, and her personal union with the spirit world...Her stone carvings embody her memory of her own wild consciousness, her union with the natural instinctual life."
~ Clarissa Pinkola Estes

Among the many truths revealed to me on my journey, I discovered that when you have taken the steps to demystify what you once perceived as your unknown wilderness then the reconnection with your wild essence brings the riches of treasured inner resources to light as well. The inner riches of your natural instincts and your creative abilities strengthen. You unearth wells of self-love, compassion and unlimited potential. You unleash traces of authenticity that hold a unique energetic vibration to anyone else in the Universe, resonating at the frequency of your authentic essence. These gifts, virtues and resources are meant to serve you in your life. They support your life purpose. They serve you in positive ways. In addition, Life will show you time and time again that the dreams and treasures embedded in your heart are also your gifts to the world.

Unearthing your treasures comes about by cultivating a consistent connection with your essential self and by creating space for this inner wilderness to exist in your life. These inner treasures or aspects of yourself, that have been suppressed and shut away in dark dusty corners need the permission to be. They need the space to breathe. This is the only way that these remnants of your wild essence can truly blossom. How do you go about doing so? By finding ways to draw out and ignite your inner wilderness. How you do that is largely determined by what resonates with you individually. The things that awaken your wild essence are unique to you. You will recognize them when they show up because of the way they kindle your spirit. Regularly engaging in activities that stimulate your inner wilderness invites it to emerge more. Cultivating a regular practice is therefore important. So is being both disciplined and consistent in maintaining that practice. In A Woman's Book of Yoga, authors Machelle Seibel and Hari Kaur Khalsa discuss the process of transformation through Kundalini yoga. They highlight that the first stage of this transformational process is called Sadhana, which means the practice of discipline. Seibel and Khalsa say that the first step to transforming yourself through yoga *"is to simply keep your word to practice every day."* In other words, making a commitment to yourself to show up every time. Set aside time and make room to connect with your wild essence regularly and then commit to consistently showing up for yourself. This concept makes me think of my grandmother. For as long as I can remember, I watched how she maintained a daily soulful meditation and prayer ritual every morning and every evening. Her spiritual practice stimulated her wild essence and allowed her to surrender the troubles of her mind, seek guidance and be at peace with who and where she was in her life. Watching her taught me that showing up and making room for the things that soothe your inner wilderness keeps you grounded and at peace. It replenishes your inner resources.

For centuries, sages, shamans, medicine women and keepers of the feminine mystical arts have dedicated time and sometimes their lives to their daily practices by means of rituals and ceremony. In recent times, rituals or ceremonies have gotten a bad rap because they've lost their relevance in today's world or have become devoid of meaning. In some instances, outmoded traditions and religious systems use rituals or ceremony to continue to suppress or keep people stuck in the lower vibrational energies of fear, which in turn taint's our perceptions of the role of ritual. But ritual and ceremony can play a positive role in nurturing your wild essence. Since the soul understands and sometimes communicates through the language of symbols, rituals and ceremonies are symbolic ways of gathering together subconscious parts of your wild essence and bringing them to the fore. Approaching such activities with mindfulness allows you to focus your intentions, to imbue them with the resonance of your loving essence and to ensure that they are meaningful. Soulful rituals and mindful routines can include anything from having a morning tea meditation ritual, to lighting a candle as you sit down to mindfully journal or having a weekly pamper session to soothe your body, mind and soul. For me, I know that the wild Earth ignites my spirit. So spending time meditating in the garden daily, as well as going on Nature walks a few times a week, nurtures my wild essence. Since I follow the cycles of the moon, I use the New Moon and Full Moon periods to become spiritually centered by participating in soulful rituals that bring me back to myself and help me to focus my intentions on attracting things or situations that inspire me. I also love tea. So I have a special tea time routine where I sit in the garden with a freshly brewed cup of tea and am just present with myself.

What makes your wild essence come alive? How can you craft daily or weekly rituals that stimulate your inner wilds to bring more of your precious self to the fore? The space that you create for your wild essence, the rituals, moments of mindfulness and vibe triggers are just as much like the thread that Adriane used to guide Theseus in and out of the cave as the regular practices of meditation or journaling mentioned in Chapter 2. These threads too lead you back to your inner wilderness every time. They are your connection to your heart space and to your feminine intuition, that inner knowing that steers you through the wild plains of your soul and this life. Below are a few ideas that you can draw on to help ignite your wild essence.

♥

Practical Ways to Give Your Wild Essence Space

Select a Wild Essence Theme Song: I first came across the idea of a theme song when I read Denise Linn's Soul Coaching book. I absorbed this idea into the Spirit Wilding e-Course that I facilitate by encouraging participants to select a wild spirit theme song to listen to every day for the duration of the course. This awesome activity helps to set the tone for the Spirit Wilding experience. Your 'Wild Essence Theme Song' can be your favorite song, something that is relevant to you right now or simply a song that ignites the wild and wondrous Spirit within. Once you've selected the song, play it every morning when you wake up. Sing along and shake your booty too if you like. Have fun as you connect with your wild essence through the music.

Vibe Triggers: Vibe triggers are points of focus that help to keep stimulating the wild energies that you've been activating on this journey. Early in this Chapter, I mentioned ancient rock paintings on the cave walls that seemed so familiar. Your vibe triggers are exactly like that – little reminders or things that you surround yourself with to activate your essential self. Vibe triggers that I like to use include, journaling, connecting with Nature, mantras, creating sacred spaces and meditation alters, reading inspiring stories, prose or poetry, among other things. All of these activities are entry points too your inner wilderness. What kinds of things activate your wild energies? Explore them and then find ways to accommodate them in your daily life wherever possible, as often as possible.

Create Wild Essence Pearls: While I was packing up my life and moving house, I realized that I had several journals with pages full of wisdom and insights. As I went through my old journals, I was in awe of the inner wisdom that found its way to these pages. Yet, I also realized that once I'd written these insights and guidance down, I often forget about them. I was left feeling that I had to find a better way to integrate this wisdom more fully. Then a while later, I came across Jenn Morrow's inspiring e-book, 'Vocalize: Five Soulful Steps for Writing from your Center'. In the e-book, she introduces a step she referred to as 'Pearls'. Morrow suggests that you read through your soulful writing, unearth the diamonds or pearls in the writing and then write them on flash cards. She then suggests stringing these pearls together into meaningful sentences or paragraphs. I immediately fell in love with the idea and have had a field day applying it in my own way. I feel that in doing so, I found yet another way to invite Spirit into my life. I made room for answers and vibe triggers to find me. It has also allowed the initial seeds planted to be watered, nurtured and to start growing into even greater insights and understanding. Find your treasures, integrate them into your life in fun ways and draw on their energy in exciting ways.

Creating Sacred Space: We all need space to retreat sometimes. Creating a sacred space helps to nurture your soul, but it can also be used as a vibe trigger when you make sacred space this allows your inner wilderness to surface. So, just as you create a space for stillness to access your inner peace, you can also create a sacred space that liberates your wild essence that allows you to release shackles or to awaken your untamed energy. Find a room, a nook or a space in your home or garden where you can connect with your inner essence. Use candles, scents, imagery and colors that stimulate. Play your wild essence song in this space and also feel free to add plants, some flowers, pebbles and feathers to draw in the wild energies of the Earth.

♥

~ Mantra Moment ~

*(Tweet, Instagram, Share on Facebook
#wildessence #jodiskyrogers)*

♥

**"I return to the peace of my wild essence
when I am centered in stillness."**

♥

**"I surrender my fear of the unknown
and embrace my inner wilderness."**

♥

**"I quiet my mind and honor the
Divine intelligence within me."**

♥

**"I find peace and freedom in the
stillness of my wild essence."**

♥

Meditation: Unearth Your Wild Treasures

Take a deep breath, in and out. Be present. Relax and be at peace in this moment.

See yourself sitting around a camp fire in the middle of a desert surrounded by small mountains. The red sand is below you. Overhead the stars burn brightly and twinkle against the black night sky. Take in the smell of the fire wood as it crackles under the heat of the dancing flames. You hear wolves howling in the distance, as if singing to the music. You hear the call of the owls.

Something at the foot of a nearby mountain catches your eye. You see a light flickering in the dark. You get up and walk toward the light. When you reach it, you see that it is coming from an opening at the mountain foot, as you get closer. It is an entrance to a dark cave.

Just when you start to feel uneasy, you notice that there are two beautiful luminous angels guarding the cave entrance. They radiate so much loving light and you feel completely at easy because you know that you are protected.

You enter the cave and notice the cave getting bright with each step that you take. Soon you find yourself around a warm fire within the cave. You sit down beside the fire.

Looking around, you see ancient rock paintings on the cave walls. This place feels so familiar, as if you have been here before.

Walk over to one of the cave walls. You notice a gap in the wall. Something tells you to reach into a hidden crevice and when you do you pull out a shining little treasure box. It is a beautiful white box with intricate carvings on it. Again, something about the box feels so familiar and you know that there is something important inside it.

The voice of your wild essence whispers: *"This belongs to you. Inside are the forgotten parts of your wild soul, inner treasures that you've kept hidden from the world."*

Sit down by the fire with your treasure box with you. Study its detail. It has carvings of flowers, trees, angels and faeries.

The treasure box emanates a vibrant and powerful energy that immediately lifts your vibration and leaves your aura buzzing.

Take a deep breathe, in and out as you honor the contents of your treasure box. Gently lift the lid and open it. You feel a wave of positive healing energy wash over you and opening your heart spaces. As you do this you know that something profound is happening.

Look inside the box. There is a tiny golden cauldron. There are also 3 tiny glass bottles with luminous elixirs. Each bottle has a label on it, indicating what it is. These bottles contain the disowned or suppressed aspects of your wild self that you would like to reclaim.

Pick up the first bottle. What part of you does it contain? Are you ready to reclaim this aspect of your beautiful wild essence? Examine the contents of the remaining bottles.

Now take your golden cauldron and pour the elixirs into it. Swirl the cauldron, bless the contents and then drink it slowly. As you do, feel your aura expanding. Feel your inner wilderness expanding, reclaiming these forgotten places within you. The precious treasures of your heart are being restored. You feel uplifted, whole and complete. You feel fierce, confident and wild.

Thank your wild essence for leading you to these treasures. Ask her if there is any guidance that she has to share with you. Listen to her answer. Thank her for her guidance.

Know that you are welcome to return to this cave to search for treasures and work with the alchemy of your treasure box as often as you want. You know where to find it now.

You are now ready to leave the cave. Stand up and walk back to the entrance. Outside the cave, look up at the stunning blanket of stars overhead. Breathe in the cool night air, in and out.

Return your attention to your body.

When you are ready, open your eyes.

> **"As he was about to climb yet another dune,**
> **his heart whispered, "Be aware of the place**
> **where you are brought to tears. That's where**
> **I am, and that's where your treasure is."**
> **~ Paulo Coelho**

6

RESTORING THE REST OF THE WILD FOREST

*"The clearest way into the Universe is
through a forest wilderness."*
~John Muir

This morning I awoke to the sound of my husband whispering my name.

"Jodi," he said in his usual gentle manner. *"Look at that…"*

I looked up at the balcony's French doors and outside I saw the first signs of morning as the fire of life set the horizon ablaze in luminous shades of gold and burnt orange. I gasped at its beauty and my heart opened. How blessed I felt to bear witness to another crimson dawn birthed over Africa, the last star still sparkling against the indigo remnants of night.

"Oh, Wow!" are the only words that I managed to turn out at the sight of what the expert hand of Mother Nature seemed to be painting before me.

"It's so beautiful, isn't it!" he said as he pulled me closer into the warmth of his tender embrace. We watched for a while as the dam waters quickly turned a liquid gold reflecting the light of the rising sun. I reveled in gratitude for our last morning here, waking up in this wonderful place – a log cabin immersed in the natural world of mystery where we'd been able to see the wild Earth awaken to the golden first breath of a new day. The past four days have been therapeutic and refreshing for us both. We came at the right time, in the last days of July, the dead of winter, just when our souls needed restoration most. Having a break to breathe through the halfway point of the year has allowed me time to take stock and review where life is going. I've had space to deepen the internal dialogue with my wild essence too. Without television, laptops or other distractions, our days here have been filled with warm winter sun, reading and simply being. It's been uplifting to have a lot more time to meditate and journal daily. Our nights here have been pretty precious too. We lit a wood fire in the cabin every evening and set a pair of wicker chairs at the French doors where we sat with the lights off and the curtains open, looking out at the night. We drank wine and shared a box of decadent chocolates while trading stories and talking about nothing and everything. It amazes me that we never run out of things to talk about and that every time we go away together we find new ways to open up to one another. A few days before we left for our trip, I found a T.S Eliot

anthology, 'The Waste Land and Other Poems', at a second hand bookstore. Cyrus studied it in high school and loves T.S Eliot's work. So he's been reading to me from the book each night while we stargaze. I love the sound of his voice and am always lost in a special place of bliss when he reads poetry to me. But hearing how he comes alive when he reads Eliot is a special treat for it is a window into the mystical essence of the wild creature that dwells within him. These words that he shares with me clearly connected with that place in his youth and now they seem to have reached across the distance of time to retrieve and resuscitate landscapes of his inner wilderness that have been dormant for a while. These are precisely the times that so plainly demonstrate the fact that poetry is a sacred language of the soul.

Last night, we decided to take a walk outside along the edge of the dam to get a better look at the stars. The tapestry of night cloaking the landscape sparkled with bright clusters of diamonds laid out in swirls and patches of little milky galaxies. The only fitting reaction to the scene was to inhale an awestruck gasp, and then exhale dreamy eyes fixed on the wonder of Great Mother Earth's evening gown. We miss so much living in the city where light pollution stultifies the appearance of the evening sky. What we saw here was breath-taking. Around us, night came alive with its nocturnal critters and sounds. Bats and moths were on the wing, flapping, gliding and diving through the chilly winter air. The bats screeched intermittently, which was both unnerving and enchanting somehow. The water rippled in the darkness, the waning moon reflecting on the surface near its edge. Cyrus put his arms around me to shield me from the cold. We stood looking up at the sky. The sense of magic around us was tangible when in a short space of time we saw four shooting stars dancing across the heavens. It had been many years since either of us had seen shooting stars. It's a small wonder that the ancients were so enthralled by these heavenly bodies. I could feel my husband's excitement. He loves starry skyscapes just as much as I do. They draw out the dreamer in him and capture his imagination. Instantaneously, his eyes lit up. In no time, he was talking about space travel, interstellar voyages and all the dreams, stories and ideas that the stars ignite in him. He has been inspired by science fiction since childhood and is obsessed with everything to do with it from sci-fi movies, to books and graphic novels. He is a gifted storyteller and writer too, so ideas for his own short stories are always swimming about in the ethers. When I watch this side of him, the wild dreamer and inspired creator, I can't help but be inspired as well, because this is the real him, the passionate person who surfaces when all the defenses and shackles are surrendered. This is the unedited version of his soul. I am honored to get to experience it.

There is something else that happens when we are at peace with our wild essence and feel free enough be who we are or when we are comfortable enough to share our inner treasures too. We catalyze the same reaction in others around us. We inspire them. We seduce them into being at ease so that they too shed their own shackles and allow their inner wilderness to surface. We become a mirror of divine wildness to them, and they inevitably respond in the same way.

The idea of this often makes me think about those fragile moments many years ago when I first met my husband. At the time, I was not used to receiving affection or positive reinforcement. A childhood plagued with bullies and growing up in a harsh environment led me to retreat inward as a defense mechanism. But something shifted when he opened the petals of his heart before me and radiated a kind and genuine love that I never thought I'd find. His honesty, warmth and openness softened the rough edges of my jaded heart, so that with time I began to open up too. This doesn't just happen in romantic connections. I feel that all human connections have the power to do this. We have the power to touch, and inspire, and restore one another. So many people walk difficult paths and often all they need is a little bit of positive energy, understanding and sincerity to encourage them to let their guard down and share the rich contents of their inner world. By being who you are more fully, openly expressing your wild essence and sharing your gifts, you inevitably give the people around you permission to let down their facades and to be themselves more freely. They open up and the pathways to meaningful connections are formed. I've come to treasure those precious moments when the other person suddenly lights up and feels comfortable and inspired enough to bring their exquisite inner self to the surface. Watching a liberated heart sparkle in plain sight is so rewarding. One never knows the burdens that each person carries or how long they have been imprisoned in the shadows of fear or pain. We've learnt to hide these parts of ourselves so well, quietly living in shame and pretending that all is fine. Yet, so many of us go through similar experiences. When you unwrap and share your wild stories, you allow others who live similar stories to know that they are not alone. When you share your dreams, you allow others to dream too. When you communicate messages of love and inspiration, you touch the lives of those who are willing to receive those messages positively.

♥

Once the sun rose, I got out of bed, threw on my favorite nightgown, a cream satin kimono with black floral prints on it and went to put the kettle on to make a cup of peppermint tea. I've made tea a part of my daily meditation ritual. I love the variety, exotic aromas and adventure that every new flavor and type of tea brings. I love that it can be healing, soothing or energizing depending on what you need. But most importantly, I love that it allows me to imbue a potentially mundane act with meaningful intentions by becoming present. With my tea, I gathered my journal and meditation crystals and went out onto the balcony. I sat at the picnic table and meditated for a few moments before mindfully sipping my tea as I journalled. A Blackheaded Oriole landed on a high branch of the pine tree directly in front of me. At first glance it looked very much like a weaver. Upon closer inspection though, one finds that although its body is covered with a similar kind of yellow feather to the weavers, its head is a stark black with piercing red eyes and its beak a bright orange. He gave two "kweeer" "kweeeeer" calls as if to say "*Good Morning*". From my writing spot on the balcony, I had the perfect view of the bird. He perched for a while and then flew off to his companion in another tree a short distance from my log cabin.

On the other side of the trout dam, I heard the sound of the forest as a gust of wind rushed over.

"*The forest…oh the forest*," I thought to myself writing my morning musings.

It's been a bearer of so many exquisite blessings. We've spent our mornings here taking forest walks and exploring every corner of it. It was made up of a mix of pines, eucalyptus, blue gums and acacia trees. Yesterday, as we entered the forest at a section of pines, it was as if a golden carpet of fallen needles rolled out before our feet. I felt honored that the wild Earth would be so kind to weave such delicate beauty for us to tread on. The forest was full of intricate textures, the canopy top reaching for the sun, the artwork of peeling bark, fallen branches, dark green undergrowth and mosses, scattered brown leaves and pine corns. It's a splendid mesh of chaotic loveliness, coupled with soothing sounds and the earthy scents of wildness. I loved the sound of the wind blowing through the trees and watching them sway from side to side as Cyrus and I walked under them. It's like music, a special language of trees that only the seasoned ear can understand. I imagine that the birds we've seen flying amongst the tree branches, the rabbits, the buck, as well as other unseen creatures of the forest have learnt to interpret it. I found myself wondering if the passing breezes allow the forest trees to experience different worlds. If the wind has travelled far and wide, coming in from the ocean miles away in the East, or from across the Savannah and bushveld North of here, do the trees get a taste of these distant lands when they dance with the passing gusts? Perhaps one day, with enough deep practice, I too will understand the language of the wind and forests more deeply.

For the moment I remained in awe of the forest energy, the community of the trees, all its inhabitants and the cloudless azure winter sky overhead on a windy morning. After spotting buck droppings and spores for a couple of days, yesterday I finally stumbled across an elusive young buck. We were walking along collecting fallen sticks and pine corns, when we noticed that some of the sticks had randomly falling into the shape of crosses. It gave us an eerie feeling and I wondered if somehow the forest was letting us know that the ground here was holy. Then minutes later and a few paces forward, we spotted it. The young buck seemed to be eating low hanging new leaf growths from a tree. Just as soon as we spotted it, the buck turned to give us a quick glance. She spooked and swiftly bolted off in the elegantly graceful manner that only young buck can. I felt the warm feeling of joy stirring within.

Centuries ago, this land would have been teaming with buck and wildlife. However, so much of the land in this area has been cleared for farming and mining over the years that spotting them here is a rare treat. Although this is not an indigenous forest, it's fortunate that the owners have allowed it to grow wild somewhat with a life of its own. As a consequence of giving the forest space to become untamed, the natural wildlife has found a place to call home too. It somehow made me think that each of us is a beautiful tree in the forest of life, rooted in the essence of our own being, our branches reaching for different dreams. You are at the center of your own story and the driver of your life. At the same time all life is interconnected. The impact that you are making by re-wilding your soul goes beyond reversing the chains of damage and returning to the freedom and peace of your wild essence. Your individual efforts play a significant role in restoring the rest of the forest to its natural dignity. What you do impacts on the people around you. The people whom you share your life with, the world and Mother Nature all experience the ripple effect of your actions. Think for a moment of how you feel when you meet someone who inspires you – a role model fighting for a worthy cause, your favorite author, a successful person at the top of their game or any larger than life person who moves you. What kind of emotions do these people stir in you? These people inspire us just by living their purpose and making the choice to follow the whispers of their wild essence. You hold the potential to the same. One of our ultimate aspirations is to touch each other's lives in a meaningful way and inspire them. You will find that each time that you follow through despite your fear, not only will your life be richer for it, but so will the lives of those who you touch along the way. We are collectively realizing our full potential as individuals, as communities and as society.

It's scary when your wild essence calls you to be brave, to march to your own beat, to walk away from the madding crowd and towards the road less travelled. Instead, that aside, it's worth keeping in mind that throughout the ages of existence, Great Mother Earth and her inhabitants have experienced times when wild whispers rose from their center, calling them to a new way of being. Responding to those internal nudges, they courageously took the first steps. Guided by Divine intelligence, new aspects of their wild essence were aroused. As a result, a ripple of change that transformed the face of the earth as initiated. I love the beautiful story of the emergence of the first flower because it's a demonstration of the impact of responding to those wild whispers. It's hard to imagine a world without flowers. Yet, until approximately 130 to 140 million years ago, flowering plants did not exist. Plants existed as gymnosperms, just like Cypress, Cedar and Pine trees still do. Then, a sudden evolution arose in these plants. They slowly started merging their male and female reproductive components and began developing flowers. As if responding to the intuitive whispers of their inner intelligence, they connected with the creative essence within and brought their dormant artist out to play. The result was a burst of floral creations springing to life across the Earth. In a culmination of color and fragrance the art that they created manifested in flowers of all shapes and sizes. Their delicate petals radiate such exquisiteness it is little wonder that flowers have been deemed 'God's laughter' and 'wordless prayers of Nature.' By following the guidance of their inner essence the emergence of flowers changed the wild Earth forever. Not only did they secure the future of their own species, but they transformed habitats, secured a vast food source for almost all living creatures on the planet and became instigators and bearers of new life.

There will always be naysayers, dream slayers, detours and stumbling blocks. Voices and people who try to keep us tamed are bound to surface from time to time, ready to derail or keep you stuck in cycles of negativity. The madding crowd and sheep-like herds who live small lives following the rules of domestication always seem to attempt to reduce those who are wild and free. But with hope and courage in your spirited heart, these minor glitches have nothing on the true magnitude and magnificence of your return to the peace and freedom of your beautiful inner wilderness.

Gathering a wild tribe of supportive souls is therefore also an important step on your journey. So many dreams are made true with the support of fellow believers standing beside you, soul connections who are there to cheer you on, who believe in you and have so much faith in your ability to manifest the vision in your heart. When you set out on your journey to re-wild your spirit and return to the serenity of your wild essence, there are bound to be moments when you feel a deep need to express what you are going through, share the experiences that are unfolding through your life and the new treasures that you are unearthing. You may feel vulnerable with your heart wide open and your emotions raw. Seeking out your wild tribe is therefore vital so that you get the kind of support that you need. By tribe I mean people who are on the same wavelength as you, people who understand your experiences and shifting perspectives because they are undergoing similar shifts. Surround yourself with the kinds of people who will uplift and empower you, the kinds of people who share your enthusiasm about your re-wilding journey and your dreams. Referring back to Martha Beck's book, Finding Your Way in a Wild New World, she points out that as you set out to find these people, you will find that they are looking for you too. I've found this to be so true. The vibration of your wild essence is ringing out the song of your soul, calling them to you. It is up to you to put yourself in a space where you are able to connect with them. So explore different means of doing so. Take courses, attend workshops or talks that resonate with your wild essence. Look into finding community groups in your area. Join online communities, networks and discussion forums. Connect with bloggers, inspiring souls, writers and authors whose work resonates with you. By reaching out you make connections, expand your social circle and also expand your support system. You find other trees in the forest. You participate in a collective restoration, one where inner worlds are returned to quiet peace and the impunity of wildness.

Throughout it all, remember always that you are a wild and perfect incarnation of Divinity. From the very moment that the original breath of existence inhaled and exhaled life into being, this is the vision that the Universe had for you. You are designed for wildness, not domestic confinement. Live this truth. Return to the peace and freedom of your wild essence.

"Something will have gone out of us as a people if we ever let the remaining wilderness be destroyed ...We simply need that wild country available to us, even if we never do more than drive to its edge and look in."
~ Wallace Stegner

Bibliography

Books

Ariadne's Thread – A Workbook of Goddess Magic, Shekhinah Mountainwater, The Crossing Press Freedom, 1991

Dairy of Anais Nin, Anais Nin, Ishi Press International, 1966

Ecological Intelligence – Rediscovering Ourselves in Nature, Ian McCallum, Africa Geographic, 2005

Finding Your Way in a Wild New World, Martha Beck, Piatkus, 2012

Lady of the Butterflies, Fiona Mountain, Preface, 2009

May Cause Miracles, Gabrielle Bernstein, Hay House, 2013

Soul Coaching, Denise Linn, Hay House, 2003

Steering By Starlight, Martha Beck, Piatkus, 2008

Stillness Speaks, Eckhart Tolle, Namaste Publishing, 2003

Women Who Run with Wolves, Dr. Clarissa Pinkola Estes, Rider Books, 2008

You Can Heal Your Life, Louise L. Hay, Hay House, 2007

Articles

Adam's Calendar - http://www.michaeltellinger.com

Evolution of the First Flower – *(Source: Natural History Magazine)* - http://tinyurl.com/p2jry3d

How do Hand-Reared Wolves and Dogs Interact with Humans? – *(Source: Companion Animal Psychology)* - http://tinyurl.com/lbuukhp

Lady of the Butterflies - http://www.fionamountain.com

Wolves do not join the dance: Sophisticated aggression control by adjusting to human social signals in dogs - *(Source: Applied Animal Behavior Science):* http://tinyurl.com/ps7f78w

ACKNOWLEDGEMENTS

I offer heartfelt gratitude to you, the reader for allowing me space in your life and taking the Wild Essence journey with me.

I offer gratitude to Divine Spirit, Great Mother Earth and the Goddess for working through me to bring positive and inspiring messages to those who are willing to receive them.

I'd like to thank my husband, Cyrus Rogers, for his love and support. I thank my mother-in-law, Ava Rogers for being my biggest fan and always believing in me. I acknowledge my parents, my little brother, Llewellyn Williams and my family, and most especially my grandparents who have been my greatest spiritual teachers.

I thank and honor the four most significant wild women in my life, Rosa Blaauw, Asanda Nesindande, Nomalanga Nkosi, Pralene Schmidt and Amy Makurumidze – thank you my super awesome soul sisters and my support system for your love, acceptance and encouragement. You all inspire me. I'd also like to thank Andre and Jennifer Bimray for the gift of their friendship, their encouragement and the special times spent in the bush together. I thank all my friends who have been a positive presence in my life, especially Teya

Esterhuizen. I acknowledge and thank Anne Linn Kaland, my writing accountability buddy for inspiring me to keep going. I acknowledge Kelley Thorrington, the amazing life coach and friend who inspired me to take the leap to pursue my dreams. I also acknowledge all the healers and spiritual teachers who have played a significant role in my healing journey.

A special thank you to my tribe of Earth Angels, all the incredible like-minded souls who have shared this beautiful journey and to the Sky Fairy Whispers virtual community for your love, faith and support. I am grateful for all of you and appreciate all of your support.